Mosaic 1
Listening/Speaking

Mosaic 1

Listening/Speaking

4th Edition

Jami Hanreddy
University of Wisconsin, Milwaukee

Elizabeth Whalley
San Francisco State University

McGraw-Hill/Contemporary

A Division of The McGraw·Hill Companies

Mosaic 1 Listening/Speaking, 4th Edition

Published by McGraw-Hill/Contemporary, a business unit of The McGraw-Hill Companies, Inc., 1221 Avenue of the Americas, New York, NY 10020. Copyright © 2002, 1996, 1990, 1985 by The McGraw-Hill Companies, Inc. All rights reserved. No part of this publication may be reproduced or distributed in any form or by any means, or stored in a database or retrieval system, without the prior written consent of The McGraw-Hill Companies, Inc., including, but not limited to, in any network or other electronic storage or transmission, or broadcast for distance learning.

Some ancillaries, including electronic and print components, may not be available to customers outside the United States.

 This book is printed on recycled, acid-free paper containing 10% postconsumer waste.

4 5 6 7 8 9 0 CUS/CUS 0 9 8 7 6 5

ISBN 0-07-232953-X
ISBN 0-07-118017-6

Editorial director: *Tina B. Carver*
Series editor: *Annie Sullivan*
Developmental editor: *Annie Sullivan*
Director of marketing and sales: *Thomas P. Dare*
Project manager: *Rose Koos*
Coordinator of freelance design: *David W. Hash*
Interior designer: *Michael Warrell, Design Solutions*
Photo research coordinator: *John C. Leland*
Photo researcher: *Amelia Ames Hill Associates/Amy Bethea*
Compositor: *Eileen Wagner Design.*
Typeface: *10.5/12 Times Roman*
Printer: Von Hoffmann Graphics, Inc.

Dedication
To the memory of Fred Goldstein, Rufus Rufty Rusty Russell III, Cindy Strauss, and Gertrude and Stanley Whalley.

For Freddy, who shared my love of puns as well as the grand metaphor.
And for Joe and Gracie whose love consummately provides the context for these efforts.

The acknowledgements and photo credits for this book begin on page 199 and are considered an extension of the copyright page.

INTERNATIONAL EDITION ISBN 0-07-118017-6
Copyright © 2002. Exclusive rights by The McGraw-Hill Companies, Inc., for manufacture and export. This book cannot be re-exported from the country to which it is sold by McGraw-Hill. The International Edition is not available in North America.

www.mhcontemporary.com/interactionsmosaic

Mosaic 1

Listening/Speaking

Mosaic 1 **Listening/Speaking**

Boost Your Students' Academic Success!

Interactions Mosaic, 4ᵗʰ edition is the newly revised five-level, four-skill comprehensive ESL/EFL series designed to prepare students for academic content. The themes are integrated across proficiency levels and the levels are articulated across skill strands. The series combines communicative activities with skill building exercises to boost students' academic success.

Interactions Mosaic, 4ᵗʰ edition features

- ■ updated content
- ■ five videos of authentic news broadcasts
- ■ expansion opportunities through the Website
- ■ new audio programs for the listening/speaking and reading books
- ■ an appealing fresh design
- ■ user-friendly instructor's manuals with placement tests and chapter quizzes

In This Chapter gives students a preview of the upcoming material.

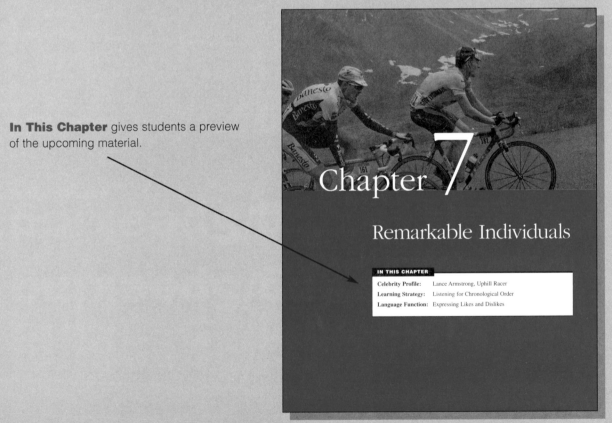

Chapter 7

Remarkable Individuals

IN THIS CHAPTER

Celebrity Profile:	Lance Armstrong, Uphill Racer
Learning Strategy:	Listening for Chronological Order
Language Function:	Expressing Likes and Dislikes

Did You Know?

- The first people to reach the South Pole were five Norwegian men led by Captain Roald Amundsen on December 4, 1911. They traveled 55 days by dog sled to get there.
- The first people to reach the North Pole were three Russian explorers who arrived and departed by air on April 23, 1968.
- The north and south polar regions balance the flow of air and water for the entire planet. Without this balance, we would face catastrophic floods and droughts (dry periods) that would change the face of the earth. In fact, if enough ice at the poles melts, an inland desert such as the one surrounding Las Vegas, Nevada, might eventually become beachfront property.

PART 1   Getting Started

Sharing Your Experience

1 Work in groups of three. Imagine that you are a zoologist about to begin a study of penguins with two other scientists. To prepare for your field study, which will include trips to Antarctica, discuss the following details with your colleagues. Write the details of your discussion in the following chart. When you are finished, compare your chart with those of other groups.

Facts about penguins we want to learn	Who we will take with us and why	Supplies needed	Where we will go first, second, etc.	How we will travel	How much time needed in each place	Dangers we will face	Times we will observe penguins

Did You Know? offers a variety of interesting facts to spark students' interest in the topic.

Part 1 Getting Started activates students' prior knowledge through prelistening questions and a vocabulary preview.

Note-taking strategies include identifying pros and cons, identifying time and sequence words, outlining, organizing information in chronological order, and listening for signal words, paraphrases, summaries, and digressions.

Listen

2 **Listening for Time and Sequence Expressions.**   Listen to the celebrity profile once all the way through. Each time you hear one of the time expressions from the explanation box, make a check mark beside it.

3 **Organizing Information in Chronological Order.**   Read the statements on the following chart. Listen to the celebrity profile again. As you listen, put an "X" in the box for the correct time frame for each statement.

Statements	During Armstrong's youth	Before he found out that he had cancer	After he found out that he had cancer	In the future
1. Armstrong won the Tour de France.			x	
2. He became an international cycling champion.				
3. He was called the "Bull from Texas."				
4. He was poor.				
5. He built up a lot of heavy muscle.				
6. He built strong and light muscles.				
7. He had a son.				
8. He was hit by a car.				
9. He wants to cross the finish line while his wife and ten children applaud.				
10. He wants to lie in a field of sunflowers.				

4. You and a friend have enrolled in a course on public relations. Unfortunately, the instructor often changes the subject and tells long and uninteresting stories about his travel adventures. You want to spend your time learning more about public relations.

To the instructor: _____

To your friend: _____

Talk It Over

4   **Discussing Goals and Interests.**

1. Look at the following chart of remarkable goals and interests. Circle those things that you would really enjoy doing and make an X through the ones you would not like to do.
2. Add other goals or interests in the blank boxes.
3. In small groups, discuss why you marked your charts the way you did. Use expressions on page 81 to express your likes and dislikes.

Arts	Sports	Home	Career	Relationships	Adventure	Other
become an artist	ride a bicycle around the world	build a house from scratch	start an Internet company	date a movie star	Climb Mt Everest	
take news photos	go bungee jumping	live on a houseboat	win the Nobel Prize for chemistry	have more than one husband or wife	travel to Antarctica	
play in a famous rock band	kick the winning goal at the World Cup Soccer Finals	have homes in New York, Paris, Tokyo, and Hong Kong	be a fashion model	have a relationship someone you meet on the Internet	ride in a hot air balloon	
sing at the opera	win an Olympic gold medal in gymnastics	live on a space station	own your own business	make friends with someone from another country	sail around the world	

Talk It Over offers a variety of speaking activities, including role-plays, interviews, presentations, small-group discussions, and pairwork.

PART 3   **Making Generalizations**

When we make statements about things that can be counted, we try to be accurate. For example:

> Of the 100 elderly people who were interviewed, 15 preferred to live with their children and grandchildren, 80 preferred to live alone, and 5 did not have a preference.

However, sometimes we may not know exact numbers. We cannot be accurate, but we do have some general ideas or opinions. In these cases we can describe what we think happens most of the time. We can *make generalizations*. Generalizations often contain adverbs of time.

Adverbs of Time in Generalizations

by and large	in general
for the most part	normally
generally	rarely
generally speaking	seldom
hardly ever	typically

1   **Comparing Expressions.** Consider these examples:

- By and large, elderly people in the United States prefer to live alone.
  Typically, the elderly in the United States enjoy living alone.

- Rock concerts are hardly ever performed in homes for the elderly.
  For the most part, rock concerts are not performed in homes for the elderly.

- Elderly women rarely compete in races.
  Generally speaking, elderly women do not compete in races.

Work in small groups. Discuss whether the two sentences in each pair of examples have the same meaning. Tell why they do or do not have the same meaning.

Language function practice takes students from identifying and understanding functional language to using it in everyday and academic settings. Some useful functions include requesting clarification, making generalizations, divulging information, using tag questions, and stating reasons.

Groupwork maximizes opportunities for discussion and negotiation.

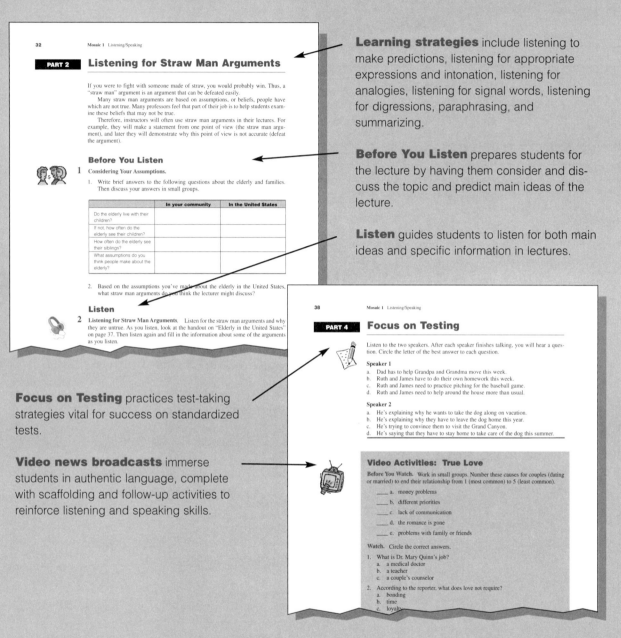

Learning strategies include listening to make predictions, listening for appropriate expressions and intonation, listening for analogies, listening for signal words, listening for digressions, paraphrasing, and summarizing.

Before You Listen prepares students for the lecture by having them consider and discuss the topic and predict main ideas of the lecture.

Listen guides students to listen for both main ideas and specific information in lectures.

Focus on Testing practices test-taking strategies vital for success on standardized tests.

Video news broadcasts immerse students in authentic language, complete with scaffolding and follow-up activities to reinforce listening and speaking skills.

Within the image:

32 Mosaic 1 Listening/Speaking

PART 2 **Listening for Straw Man Arguments**

If you were to fight with someone made of straw, you would probably win. Thus, a "straw man" argument is an argument that can be defeated easily.

Many straw man arguments are based on assumptions, or beliefs, people have which are not true. Many professors feel that part of their job is to help students examine these beliefs that may not be true.

Therefore, instructors will often use straw man arguments in their lectures. For example, they will make a statement from one point of view (the straw man argument), and later they will demonstrate why this point of view is not accurate (defeat the argument).

Before You Listen

1 **Considering Your Assumptions.**

1. Write brief answers to the following questions about the elderly and families. Then discuss your answers in small groups.

	In your community	In the United States
Do the elderly live with their children?		
If not, how often do the elderly see their children?		
How often do the elderly see their siblings?		
What assumptions do you think people make about the elderly?		

2. Based on the assumptions you've made about the elderly in the United States, what straw man arguments do you think the lecturer might discuss?

Listen

2 **Listening for Straw Man Arguments.** Listen for the straw man arguments and why they are untrue. As you listen, look at the handout on "Elderly in the United States" on page 37. Then listen again and fill in the information about some of the arguments as you listen.

38 Mosaic 1 Listening/Speaking

PART 4 **Focus on Testing**

Listen to the two speakers. After each speaker finishes talking, you will hear a question. Circle the letter of the best answer to each question.

Speaker 1
a. Dad has to help Grandpa and Grandma move this week.
b. Ruth and James have to do their own homework this week.
c. Ruth and James need to practice pitching for the baseball game.
d. Ruth and James need to help around the house more than usual.

Speaker 2
a. He's explaining why he wants to take the dog along on vacation.
b. He's explaining why they have to leave the dog home this year.
c. He's trying to convince them to visit the Grand Canyon.
d. He's saying that they have to stay home to take care of the dog this summer.

Video Activities: True Love

Before You Watch. Work in small groups. Number these causes for couples (dating or married) to end their relationship from 1 (most common) to 5 (least common).

_____ a. money problems

_____ b. different priorities

_____ c. lack of communication

_____ d. the romance is gone

_____ e. problems with family or friends

Watch. Circle the correct answers.

1. What is Dr. Mary Quinn's job?
    a. a medical doctor
    b. a teacher
    c. a couple's counselor

2. According to the reporter, what does love not require?
    a. bonding
    b. time
    c. loyalty

Don't forget to check out the new *Interactions Mosaic* Website at www.mhcontemporary.com/interactionsmosaic.

- Traditional practice and interactive activities
- Links to student and teacher resources
- Cultural activities
- Focus on Testing
- Activities from the Website are also provided on CD-ROM

Speaking Tasks	Focus on Testing	Lecture Topics	Video Topics
■ Sharing new experiences ■ Making predictions ■ Role-playing predictions ■ Discussing clarifications ■ Requesting clarification ■ Solving brain teasers	■ Getting meaning from context	■ Learning to Speak Someone Else's Language	■ An Exchange Student
■ Talking about how you spend your time ■ Discussing main ideas in conversations ■ Asking for confirmation in a lecture ■ Asking for confirmation in a project presentation ■ Making excuses	■ Getting meaning from context	■ Learning to Listen/ Listening to Learn	■ High-Tech Jobs and Low-Tech People
■ Discussing the elderly and families/sharing assumptions ■ Interviewing community members about family life ■ Generalizing about families	■ Getting meaning from context	■ Family Networks and the Elderly	■ True Love
■ Comparing body parts to objects ■ Discussing the heart ■ Setting contexts for analogies ■ Discussing and comparing analogies ■ Expressing personal opinions ■ Role-playing health situations	■ Getting meaning from context	■ What Makes Us Tick: The Cardiac Muscle	■ Bottled Water
■ Discussing space flight expenses vs. benefits ■ Using notes to recall information ■ Giving a tour of a city ■ Using the passive voice to report the news	■ Getting meaning from context	■ Space Flight: A Simulation	■ Internet Publishing
■ Discussing banks ■ Asking about the World Bank ■ Discussing pros and cons of the World Bank ■ Considering ways to invest money ■ Agreeing and disagreeing ■ Discussing current events ■ Developing an action plan	■ Getting meaning from context	■ The World Bank Under Fire	■ Welfare Payments

(continued on next page)

Speaking Tasks	Focus on Testing	Lecture Topics	Video Topics
■ Discussing remarkable people ■ Discussing the order of events ■ Completing a timeline ■ Telling a story ■ Choosing appropriate expressions and tone to express likes and dislikes ■ Discussing goals and interests	■ Getting meaning from context	■ Lance Armstrong: Uphill Racer	■ Overcoming Serious Illness
■ Discussing inventions ■ Brainstorming uses for ordinary objects ■ Using free association ■ Discussing creativity ■ Using communication signals ■ Researching and reporting on animal communication ■ Completing conversations ■ Divulging information	■ Getting meaning from context	■ Creativity: As Essential to the Engineer as to the Artist	■ A Life of Painting
■ Discussing sociability ■ Discussing and comparing digressions ■ Reporting on digressions in meetings ■ Discussing group activities ■ Using tag questions to confirm information ■ Using tag questions in role-plays	■ Getting meaning from context	■ Group Dynamics	■ People Skills
■ Discussing common wrong-doings ■ Discussing crimes and punishments ■ Discussing predermination and free will ■ Paraphrasing and discussing parts of a lecture ■ Paraphrasing and discussing problem situations ■ Expressing wishes and hopes ■ Role-playing hopes and desires	■ Getting meaning from context	■ Human Choice: Predetermination or Free Will?	■ Victim Support Groups
■ Discussing plans for a field study ■ Predicting main ideas and supporting information ■ Speaking from an outline ■ Stating reasons for and against zoos	■ Getting meaning from context	■ Penguins at the Pole	■ Air Pollution
■ Discussing humor ■ Sharing folk wisdom and advice ■ Creating sayings ■ Role-playing quotations ■ Telling jokes	■ Getting meaning from context	■ Folk Wisdom	■ An Endangered Species

Chapter 1

New Challenges

Did You Know?

- Dr. Harold Williams holds the record for speaking the most languages. He was a journalist from New Zealand who lived from 1876 to 1928. He taught himself to speak 58 languages and many dialects fluently.

- The language with the most letters is Khmer, which used to be called Cambodian. It has 74 letters. The Rotokas of Papua, New Guinea, have the language with the fewest letters. It has only 11 letters (*a, b, e, g, i, k, o, p, r, t,* and *v*).

- The most complicated language in the world may be the language spoken by the Inuit peoples of North America and Greenland. It has 63 different types of present tense, and some nouns have up to 250 different forms.

PART 1

Getting Started

Sharing Your Experience

Think about the following questions and make a few brief notes to help you remember your thoughts. Then discuss your answers as a class or in small groups.

1 Someone once said that getting to know a person is like peeling an onion. Have you ever peeled an onion? How might this be like getting to know a person?

_____

_____

2 Have you ever traveled to a new place or been to a party where you didn't know anyone? Did you find yourself behaving differently than normal? Try to recall an experience like this or try to imagine yourself in this situation. Include answers to these questions.

1. *Where* were you?   _____

2. *What* did you do?   _____

3. *Why* did you do it?   _____

4. Is it sometimes easier to talk about yourself with people who don't know you? Why or why not?

_____

_____

3 Has your study of English changed you in any way? If so, how? Share your answers to the following questions and give specific examples.

1. How has it made you more or less outgoing?

_____

2. How has it made you more or less critical of how people speak your native language?

_____

3. How has it made you more or less tolerant of other cultures?

_____

4. How has it changed your understanding or opinion of human nature?

_____

Vocabulary Preview

4 **Determining Meaning from Context.** You will hear the underlined words in the following sentences in the lecture. Write the letter of the correct definition beside each sentence.

Noam Chomsky, a famous linguist, suggested that the ability to learn a language is innate

Sentences	Definitions
___ 1. The professor looked at the <u>collage</u> made of paper, wood, leaves, and glue that was hanging on the wall of his office.	a. connection (in the mind)
___ 2. This all looks so familiar. I feel that we've been here before. I guess it must just be <u>déjà vu</u>.	b. to change the nature of something
___ 3. As a famous <u>linguist</u>, he is interested in the study of language acquisition.	c. an artistic creation of materials and objects glued onto a surface
___ 4. Language presents us with a <u>paradox</u>; it helps us communicate, but communication is not possible if two people speak different languages.	d. accept or agree with someone's point of view
___ 5. For a long time, researchers thought we learned language through <u>imitation</u> of others and <u>association</u> of words.	e. person who studies the nature and structure of human language
___ 6. If we speak French <u>fluently</u>, we can begin to see the world from a French point of view.	f. something overly familiar; a feeling of having had an experience before
___ 7. Learning to speak someone else's language can <u>transform</u> us.	g. present at birth; natural
___ 8. I'm not sure I <u>buy</u> that idea.	h. statement/situation that presents opposing views as true at the same time
___ 9. Noam Chomsky, a famous linguist, suggested that the ability to learn a language is <u>innate</u>.	i. modeling one's behavior or speech on the behavior or speech of another person
	j. spoken or written effortlessly and naturally

Listening to Make Predictions

Surprises can be nice in everyday life, but if they occur frequently in a lecture, the lecture may be difficult to understand. In order not to be surprised too often, it is useful to anticipate what the instructor will say next. Here are two guidelines to help you make predictions:

1. Before you listen to the lecture, think about what you already know and what you want to learn about the topic.
2. As you listen to the lecture, predict what the speaker will say. When the lecturer makes a statement:
    a. Predict what she or he will say next.
    b. Judge quickly whether you were right or wrong.
    c. If you were right, move on to your next prediction.
    d. If you were wrong, don't worry about it, or you'll miss the next part of the lecture. Just put a question mark in your notes for clarification later and move on to the next prediction.

When you focus your listening in this way, you are less likely to be distracted by thoughts of things such as lunch, your soccer game, or the date you had Saturday night.

Before You Listen

1   **Discussing the Topic.**   Write brief answers to the following questions. Discuss your answers in small groups.

1. What do you already know about the topic "Learning to Speak Someone Else's Language?"

_____

_____

2. What do you think the speaker will discuss?

_____

_____

3. What questions do you have on the topic?

_____

_____

Listen

2   **Listening to Make Predictions.**   Listen to the lecture one section at a time. This will give you the opportunity to understand what has been said already and to predict what will come next. The quotes from the lecture indicate where you should stop the lecture.

Stop 1   *Just call out your questions.*

Predict what questions you think the students will ask.

_____

_____

Stop 2   *Then let's begin with that last question. Can we ever really learn to speak another person's language?*

Did you predict some of the questions the students asked? What do you think the professor's answer will be to that last question? Why?

_____

_____

Stop 3   *Now this brings us back to the first question on our list: Where does language come from? And how does it develop?*

What do you think the professor's answer will be to this question?

_____

_____

Stop 4   *Chomsky suggested that this accomplishment is possible because human babies have an innate ability to learn any language in the world.*

Have you ever heard of Chomsky? Do you believe that humans have an innate ability to learn language? What will the professor discuss next?

_____

_____

Stop 5   *. . . our native language actually determines the way we see the world.*

What does this statement mean? What kind of examples do you think the professor might give?

_____

_____

Stop 6   *English sometimes uses words from other languages to express a thought or name a thing in a better way.*

What are some words that the professor might use as examples here?

_____

_____

After You Listen

3   **Comparing Predictions.**   Listen to the lecture again. At each of the stops, compare your predictions with those of your classmates. Were you able to make accurate predictions? What did you learn from your classmates' predictions?

Talk It Over

4 **Making Predictions.**   For each of the following situations, predict what you think will occur. Follow these three rules:

1. Don't tell anyone your predictions.
2. Write what you think will happen in the spaces following each situation.
3. Predict whether the characters will communicate well ("speak each other's language") or whether they will have a misunderstanding.

1. Characters
Character 1: A short man, about 65 years old
Character 2: A tall woman, about 75 years old

Situation
The woman and man are standing in front of the only empty seat on a crowded New York City subway. If the man sits down, he is being impolite. If he stands up, he may fall because he is too short to reach the strap.

Your prediction:

Example: _The woman convinces the man to sit down. They start talking. Both of them miss their stops. They communicate well and agree to get off the subway at the next stop and have coffee together._

Example: _The man gives the seat to the woman. When the subway starts suddenly, he falls into her lap. They communicate well and they laugh and say that there should be more subways during rush hour._

Example: _The man and the woman see the seat at the same time. They do not communicate well and while they are arguing, someone else comes along and takes the seat._

2. Characters
Character 1: A 16-year-old man who wants to be a rock musician. He is kind and loves his mother. His father died when he was a small boy.
Character 2: A loving but very conservative mother

Situation
The young man wants to have his nose pierced, but he only wants to do it with his mother's permission. The mother and son are sitting in the living room discussing the pros and cons of piercing.

Your prediction:

_____

_____

3. Characters

Character 1: A shy young man, 26 years old

Character 2: A confident young woman, 25 years old

Situation

The young man and young woman met a year and a half ago. She would like to marry him. He would like to marry her. They're finishing a romantic dinner at a very nice restaurant. Both the young man and the young woman are trying to figure out a way to bring up the topic of marriage.

Your prediction:

_____

_____

4. Characters

Character 1: Harry, 22 years old, who has two tickets to a soccer match

Character 2: Bob, 22 years old, who has a passion for soccer and a chemistry midterm exam tomorrow

Situation

Bob and Harry are in a coffee shop at 3:00 P.M. Harry is trying to convince Bob to go to the soccer match.

Your prediction:

_____

_____

5. Characters

Character 1: A student who is buying food for a party

Character 2: A grocery store clerk, a student and friend of Character 1

Situation

The first student is at the checkout counter of the store with $83 worth of drinks and food for a party. He finds he has only $64 cash with him. The store will not accept checks or credit cards. The clerk at the store is a close personal friend of the student but has not yet been invited to the party.

Your prediction:

_____

_____

6. Characters

Character 1: A freshman named Jane at Needles College, who is not athletic at all and always makes jokes about exercising

Character 2: A freshman named Alice at Red River College, who is very athletic and jogs every day

Situation

Before the two young women went off to college in September, Jane said, "I bet I'll lose ten pounds by November 15th and you won't." Each young woman placed inside an envelope a secret note that said, "If I lose ten pounds and you don't, you have to _____". Now it is November 15th. First the young women open the envelopes and read the notes. Then they each get on the scale.

Your prediction (include what each woman wrote in her secret note):

_____

_____

7. Characters

Character 1: A father living in Chicago

Character 2: His 15-year-old son

Situation

The father has been offered a good job with higher pay in Toronto and wants to move. But his son does not want to leave Chicago, his high school, and all his friends. They are discussing this problem at breakfast.

Your prediction:

_____

_____

8. Characters

Character 1: An "A" student who has just gotten a failing grade for the first time on a midterm exam

Character 2: A professor who is tough but usually fair

Situation

The student is in the professor's office, explaining why he or she failed the exam. The student tells the professor about a personal problem and asks to take the exam again.

Your prediction:

_____

_____

9. Characters

Character 1: The father of a 3-day-old baby

Character 2: The mother of the baby

Situation

The local laws require that parents choose a name for their baby after three days. The mother wants to name the baby Sunshine; the father hates that name and wants to name the baby Hester, after his mother.

Your prediction:

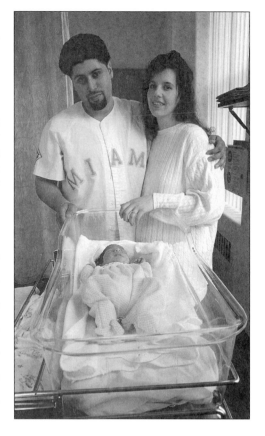

_____

_____

_____

_____

_____

_____

10. Characters

Character 1: Maria, an art student who has just moved into a new apartment

Character 2: Rob, a business major and a good friend of Maria's

Situation

Maria is in her new apartment, hanging pictures on the wall. The doorbell rings and Rob walks in with a gift, a picture for Maria's apartment. Maria thinks it is the ugliest picture she has ever seen.

Your prediction:

_____

_____

5 **Role-Plays.**

1. Work with a partner. Choose one of the previous ten situations to act out.
2. Allow about 10 to 12 minutes to prepare a role-play. You may use the prediction that you wrote for the situation, the one your partner wrote, or write a new one together.
3. Present your role-play to the class.
4. After each pair of students presents a role-play, share the predictions you wrote about that situation.

   ■ Did anyone in the class predict what happened in the role-play?
   ■ Were your predictions similar, or were they different? If there were similarities, why do you think they happened?
   ■ If there were different predictions, do you think your individual perspectives (your personal languages) account for the differences? Discuss why or why not.

PART 3 # Offering and Requesting Clarification

We all have noticed that sometimes people don't seem to be following what we are saying. They might look confused, uncomfortable, nervous, or even tense as they try to understand. Listeners who are not following what we are saying may not be paying attention or may be bored.

Ways to Offer Clarification

One way to make sure that people understand what we are saying is to offer clarification when it is needed. To do this, we can either repeat the information exactly or say it again in another way using different words.

Expressions to Offer Clarification

Appropriate for most situations

- Are you following me?
- Are you with me?
- Did you get that?
- Do you understand so far?
- Does that make sense to you?
- Is that clear?
- OK so far?
- Right?

Not appropriate for formal situations

- Did you catch that?
- Got it?

FYI: Listeners are usually appreciative when you use these expressions to check whether or not they need clarification. But be careful with your tone of voice. You don't want to sound as if you were angry because they weren't listening.

1 **Listening for Intonation.**   Listen for the difference in tone between a helpful question and scolding in the following conversations. Each of the speakers uses the same expression to try to find out whether the listener is following what has been said. Then answer the questions.

Conversation 1

Ms. Garcia is talking to a group of employees.

1. Which of the expressions from the explanation box does Ms. Garcia use?

_____

2. What is her intention when she uses this expression?

_____

Conversation 2

Mrs. Smith is talking to her son.

1. Mrs. Smith uses the same expression as Ms. Garcia did in Conversation 1.

2. What is Mrs. Smith's intention when she uses this expression?

_____

2   **Listening for Expressions That Offer Clarification.**   When you listened to the lecture earlier, did you notice that the lecturer used several expressions for offering clarification? Using the same expressions repeatedly is part of a lecturer's style. Being familiar with a lecturer's style can help you understand the content of the lecture.

Listen to the lecture again. This time, notice which expressions the lecturer uses to offer clarification. Each time the lecturer uses an expression, put a check next to it.

_____ Are you following me?

_____ Did you get that?

_____ Does that make sense to you?

_____ OK so far?

_____ Right?

3   **Discussion.**   Discuss these questions with your classmates.

1.   Which expressions seem to be the professor's favorite ones?
2.   Which ones doesn't he use?
3.   Did you need clarification when the professor offered it?
4.   Were there times when you needed clarification and the professor did not offer it? Which expressions would you use to ask for clarification?

Ways to Request Clarification

When you are the speaker and you see that the listener isn't following you, it is easy to be polite and offer clarification. When you are the listener, however, you cannot be certain that the speaker will know when you need clarification. Therefore, when you don't understand what someone is saying, don't wait for offers of clarification. Request information when you need it. You may have to politely interrupt the speaker.

Polite Expressions for Interrupting

One of these:	Followed by one of these:
Could/Can/May I interrupt?	Would you mind repeating that?
Excuse me.	Could/Would you repeat that please?
Pardon me.	Could/Would you say that again please?
I beg your pardon.	I didn't get the last part (word, etc.).
I'm sorry.	What was that again?

Informal Expressions for Requesting Clarification

Huh? (very informal)	What?
I didn't get the last part (word, etc.)	What did you say?
I didn't catch that	You lost me.

4   **Requesting Clarification.**   Listen to the lecture again.

■ If you are listening to the lecture during class, raise your hand when you do not understand something. Your instructor will stop the tape and you may request clarification from the instructor or from a classmate. Practice using a variety of expressions. Be ready to help your classmates when they request clarification.

■ If you are listening to the lecture by yourself, stop the tape whenever you do not understand something and practice requesting clarification. Practice using a variety of expressions. Put a check next to each expression as you practice it.

Talk It Over

5   **Brain Teasers.**   Work with a partner. Take turns being the presenter and the listener for the following challenging problems. Some of them are riddles and others are "brain teasers." As you do them, you'll understand why. (The answers are on page 148.)

1. **Presenter:** Read the problem silently, and then read the problem aloud to your partner as quickly as you can. Do not pause at all.

   Listener: Keep your book closed. Do not read along with your partner. If you do not understand something, ask for clarification. Use one of the expressions for requesting clarification.

2. **Presenter:** Read the problem again. This time, slow down a little and frequently use expressions to check if your partner needs clarification.

   Listener: Tell your partner if you still need clarification.

3. **Presenter:** Slow down even more if necessary.

   Listener: Try to solve the problem.

When you have done all the problems with your partner, compare your answers with those of your classmates.

Problems

1. How much is 1 times 2 times 3 times 4 times 5 times 6 times 7 times 8 times 9 times zero?

2. Write down this eight-digit number: 12,345,679. Multiply this number by any *one* of the eight numbers. Now multiply by 9. What did you get? Try it again, but this time multiply by another of the eight digits before you multiply by 9. What did you get this time?

3. Mary lives on the 12th floor of her apartment building. When she wants to go to her apartment, she gets into the elevator in the lobby and pushes the button for the 6th floor. When the elevator arrives at the 6th floor, she gets off and walks up the stairs to the 12th floor. Mary prefers to ride the elevator, so why does she get off and walk up the stairs?

4. Farmer Higg owns three red hens, four brown hens, and one black hen. How many of Higg's hens can say that they are the same color as another hen on Higg's farm?

5. What is it that occurs once in a minute, twice in a moment, yet not at all in a week?

6. Think of a number from 1 to 20. Add 1 to this number. Multiply by 2. Add 3. Multiply by 2. Subtract 10. Tell me the answer and I'll tell you the number you started with.

7. A man wants to cross a river. He has a lion, a sheep, and a bale of hay that he must take with him. He has a boat, but it will carry only him and one other thing. So the trouble is, if he leaves the lion alone with the sheep, the lion might eat the sheep. If he leaves the sheep alone with the hay, the sheep might eat the hay. How does he get himself, the lion, the sheep, and the hay to the other side of the river?

8. The governor of Goleta wants to give a small dinner party. He invites his father's brother-in-law, his brother's father-in-law, his father-in-law's brother, and his brother-in-law's father. How many people does he invite?

PART 4	# Focus on Testing

Understanding spoken English on standardized listening comprehension tests, such as the TOEFL, is more difficult than listening in most other contexts. During a standardized test, you cannot interact with the speaker to get clarification or rewind the tape to listen again. You get only one chance to listen for the important information. The Focus on Testing exercises in this book will help you practice this type of test.

Listen to the two speakers. After each speaker finishes talking, you will hear a question. Circle the letter of the best answer to each question.

Speaker 1

a. why he didn't get the part in the school play
b. what Dr. Jackson said yesterday
c. what kind of play a pun is
d. what Dr. Jackson just said

Speaker 2

a. Some languages are more fun to learn than others.
b. Adults and children speak the same language.
c. Some languages are disappearing from the earth.
d. Children shouldn't speak their parents' native language.

Video Activities: An Exchange Student

Before You Watch.   Discuss these questions in small groups.

1. What is an exchange student?
2. What problems do you think exchange students might have?

Watch.   Circle the correct answers.

1. Where is Adáh from?
    a. the United States
    b. Switzerland
    c. Turkey

2. Circle the kinds of problems that exchange students and their families sometimes have.
    a. money
    b. chores
    c. studying
    d. cultural/language problems

3. What kind of problem did Adáh have?
   a. Her homestay sister was jealous of her.
   b. She had to share the computer.
   c. She didn't have a good social life.

4. Who was Adáh's best friend?
   a. Jeli
   b. Corey
   c. her date

5. What happened to Adáh's best friend?
   a. She got sick.
   b. She had a car accident.
   c. She went home.

Watch Again.   Compare answers in small groups.

1. How old is Adáh? _____

2. What are the initials of the exchange student organization?
   a. EVS
   b. AFS
   c. ALS

3. Look at Adáh's report card and answer these questions.
   a. What languages is she studying?
   b. What science class is she taking?
   c. What is her average grade?

4. What percentage of exchange students goes home early or change families?
   a. 2%
   b. 12%
   c. 20%

5. Look at the chart that Adáh made of her "highs and lows." In which month did she feel the best?
   a. August
   b. September
   c. October

After You Watch. Discuss these questions in small groups.

1. Have you ever known any exchange students? What countries were they from?

2. Would you like to be an exchange student? Why or why not? Where would you like to go?

Chapter 2

Looking at Learning

Did You Know?

■ The largest university in the world is the State University of New York. In 2000, it was composed of 64 campuses across the state and had an enrollment of 367,000 students.

■ The youngest university student on record is Michael Tan of Christchurch, New Zealand. He was only 7½ years old when he passed his examinations in mathematics, which is equivalent to a high school diploma in the United States.

■ The most expensive school in the world is probably the Gstaad International School in Gstaad, Switzerland. In 1999, the yearly cost was about $93,760.

PART 1   # Getting Started

Sharing Your Experience

Do the following discussion activities in small groups.

1 **How Do You Spend Your Time?**

1. Think about how much time you spend each day sleeping, speaking, listening, reading, and writing. How much time are you awake but not communicating? Place a check under the appropriate percentage to indicate how much of each day you spend in these activities.

	0%	25%	50%	75%	100%
Sleeping:					
Speaking:					
Listening:					
Reading:					
Writing:					
Awake but not communicating:					

2. Compare your scale with those of your classmates. Are the scales similar or different? Share the reasons you marked particular percentages on your scale.

2 How Fast Do You Speak?

How fast do you think people speak? Seventy-five words per minute? One hundred twenty-five words per minute? Two hundred? Let's find out how fast your teacher and your classmates speak.

1. In three separate intervals of ten seconds each, your teacher will speak about one of his or her learning experiences. In each interval, make a mark (1111, 11, etc.) on the line for each word your teacher says. Then add up all the marks for the three intervals and multiply by two. This gives you the total number of words your teacher might speak in one minute.

    Interval 1: _____

    Interval 2: _____

    Interval 3: _____

    Total number of marks _____ x 2 = _____ number of words spoken per minute

2. In groups of three, take turns speaking about your learning experiences, as your teacher did in Activity 2. To help you organize your thoughts, make a few brief notes about these experiences before you begin.

	Student A	**Student B**	**Student C**
Interval 1			
Interval 2			
Interval 3			
Total marks (Intervals 1 + 2 + 3)			
x 2	x 2	x 2	x 2
Total words per minute			

3. Compare the results in your group with those of other groups. What is the average number of words spoken by a student in one minute? How does this compare to the number of words spoken by your teacher in one minute?

Vocabulary Preview

3   **Vocabulary in Context.**   Complete the following sentences with these words from the lecture.

counterexample	*an example that demonstrates an opposite view*
gist	*main idea*
to stick with	*to keep working on; to stay with*
uncomplicated	*simple; easy to understand*
upcoming	*going to happen in the near future*

1.   The thing I like about Professor Crawford's lectures is that they are very straightforward and completely _____.

2.   I knew the lecturer was wrong because I could easily think of a _____.

3.   What I like about Rose-Marie is that she always _____ her projects and never gives up until they are finished.

4.   "I can always get the _____ of what Professor McClellum says, but because of his Scottish accent, I never understand every word," said Taku.

5.   I'm really nervous about my _____ exam.

4   **Using Vocabulary.**   In small groups, share your answers to the following questions.

1.   "I've never even met a woman who likes math."
From your own experience, what is a good <u>counterexample</u> to this point of view?

2.   Do you think there is a difference between being a "quitter" and knowing when to quit? Do you always <u>stick with</u> everything you set out to learn? Why or why not?

3.   Do you think that learning is a complicated or an <u>uncomplicated</u> process? Explain your answer by giving a few examples.

4.   Think of a film that you have seen. What was the <u>gist</u> of it?

5.   What are one or two <u>upcoming</u> events on your calendar?

PART 2   # Listening for Main Ideas

Most lectures have a single overall main idea. It is the one idea that you can state briefly when a classmate asks you, "What was the lecture about?" In most cases, there are several other main ideas in addition to the overall one. These main ideas are the messages that the lecturer wants you to remember.

Lecturers present examples and details to support the main ideas. Facts and illustrations may come before or after the main idea that they support. It is easier to pick out main ideas and understand the lecture as a whole if you can identify the order in which the speaker is presenting main ideas and details.

Guidelines for Listening for Main Ideas

1. As you listen to a lecture, note the most important points and try to distinguish them from the details and illustrations.

2. Identify whether the lecturer is using the deductive or inductive method of presenting ideas. The deductive method starts with a main idea, followed by several examples or details that support it. The inductive method starts with the details and builds up to the main idea.

Deductive

    Main Idea 1
    Examples or Details 1
    Main Idea 2
    Examples or Details 2

Inductive

    Examples or Details 1
    Main Idea 1
    Examples or Details 2
    Main Idea 2

3. Lecturers sometimes mix these two ways of presenting information, which can be confusing. If an instructor does this, it is a good idea to rewrite your notes as soon as possible after class. Rewriting helps you identify the main ideas, distinguish them from supporting details, and clarify anything that is confusing to you.

Before You Listen

1 **Making a Guess.**   Before you listen, discuss the following questions in small groups.

1. Do you think that people understand more words than they can say in the same amount of time?

2. How many spoken words per minute do you think people can understand? Three hundred words per minute? Four hundred? Mark your guess below. Check your guess after you listen to the lecture.

I think people can understand _____ spoken words per minute.

Listen

2 **Listening for Main Ideas.** First read the details in the left column. As you listen to the lecture, fill in the main ideas in the right column. Listen to the lecture a second time to verify the main ideas.

Details	Main idea
1. a. We can reread, but we cannot "re-listen." b. We can control the speed when we read, but we can't when we listen. c. When we listen we must understand immediately, since we can't use a dictionary easily.	1. *Reading and listening are different in three ways.*
2. a. Think ahead. b. Evaluate what the speaker says. c. Review what was said.	2.
3. a. People are less likely to daydream when taking notes. b. Notes make it easier to review. c. Notes can remind you of information you have forgotten.	3.
4. a. Write only "Bee hummingbird is 2½ inches."	4.
5. a. You can review notes after dinner, before you go to sleep, or the first thing in the morning.	5.
6. a. Thesis/conclusion system b. Fact/principle system	6.

After You Listen

3 **Comparing Notes.** Compare your main ideas from Activity 2 with a partner.

Talk It Over

4 **Identifying Main Ideas in Conversations.** In addition to identifying the main ideas in lectures, we must also be able to get the gist of what is said in conversations. The main ideas expressed in a conversation may be uncomplicated statements such as:

- It was fun having the class party at Disneyland this year.
- I really don't like dormitory food.
- I admire my biology professor.

This type of statement in a conversation, just as in lectures, is usually followed or preceded by examples and details.

However, the main ideas expressed in a conversation may not always be so clear. Sometimes details are given, but a direct statement connecting these details is not. In these cases, the gist of what the person is saying often has to do with his or her personal feelings or opinions. Then the main idea can be understood only from these feelings or opinions.

Consider the following conversation between Keesha and Jared.

Jared: How's the food at the cafeteria here?

Keesha: Well, the soup is very salty, they cook the vegetables for hours, and the meat is always gray. If the food is supposed to be cold, they serve it warm; if it's supposed to be hot, they serve it cold.

What is the gist of what Keesha is saying about the cafeteria food?

_____

_____

1.   Interview students or others outside of class to find someone who has done one of the following:

   ■   attended school in a foreign country
   ■   taught a class
   ■   failed (or almost failed) a class
   ■   learned a new, very complicated skill
   ■   worked while going to school
   ■   learned how to read before they entered school
   ■   learned to speak more than one language fluently
   ■   learned something very surprising about someone they thought they knew well
   ■   learned something very surprising about themselves

2.   Ask the person to tell you about this experience. As you listen, take mental notes of the main ideas. Pay close attention in order to get the gist of what the person is saying.

3. Report back to the class about your conversations. Be sure to include the following:

  ■ a brief description of the person you spoke with and the situation you spoke about

  ■ the main ideas, the gist of the conversation

  ■ whether the gist of what the person said was stated directly or not

4. Find out if any of the people you and your classmates spoke with had similar experiences. That is, were any of the main ideas they expressed similar? If so, why?

PART 3 # Asking for Confirmation

Sometimes it is difficult to know exactly what a speaker means, even when you have heard and understood every word. When this happens, ask the speaker for confirmation of your understanding. A good way to do this is to state what you heard in your own words and then ask if you understood correctly. To confirm that you have understood without insulting the speaker, you must ask your questions carefully.

Asking for Confirmation

One of these:

■ I'm not sure I understand.

■ Professor, am I (is this) right?

■ I'm not sure I'm getting this.

■ I don't know exactly what you mean.

Followed by one of these:

■ Do you mean that ... ?

■ Are you saying ... ?

■ Is it ... ?

■ Do you mean to say that ... ?

■ Do you mean to imply that ... ?

With friends or family you can confirm something less formally by omitting the first sentence and using only one of the second sentences listed. Or you may simply ask, "You mean ... ?"

---

 1 **Listening for Appropriate Expressions and Intonation.**   Listen to the following conversations. Sometimes the expressions to ask for confirmation are used correctly and sometimes they are not. Sometimes the intonation makes the difference. Listen and answer the questions. Then discuss them with your classmates.

Conversation 1

At the side of the road, a lost driver is asking a police officer for directions.

Did the lost driver ask for confirmation appropriately? _____

Conversation 2

Here is a conversation between a professor and a student.

Did the student respond appropriately? _____

Conversation 3

Here is a similar conversation between the same professor and student.
1.   How do you feel about this student's confirmation strategy?

    _____

    _____

2.   Do your classmates feel the same way? _____

Conversation 4

In this conversation, a student is talking to an administrative assistant about the preregistration procedure.

How would you react if you were this administrative assistant?

_____

_____

Conversation 5

Here is another conversation between an administrative assistant and a student.

What is the main difference between Conversations 4 and 5?

_____

_____

_____

2   **Asking for Confirmation During a Lecture.**   Listen to the lecture again. This time, your instructor will stop the lecture so that you can ask for confirmation of your understanding. The following sentences indicate where you should stop the lecture. Each time the instructor stops the tape, practice asking for confirmation using the appropriate expressions.

Stop 1   *One-half of that time was spent listening.*

Do you mean that 50% of the time was spent listening?

Stop 2   *When we listen, the speed of the message is established by the speaker.*

Stop 3   *Actually, people can listen at a rate of 300 words per minute and not lose any comprehension.*

Stop 4   *Now he's going to talk about Newton's ideas from Chapter 2 because he's already talked about Galileo from Chapter 1.*

Stop 5   *Or you may decide to do it just before you go to sleep or the first thing in the morning.*

Stop 6   *The thesis/conclusion system works best with well-organized lectures that have an introduction, a body, and a conclusion.*

Stop 7   *Then, when you review, you can see if the principles tie together into one main concept or thesis.*

Stop 8   *And believe me, you'll get plenty of chances to practice this term.*

3   **Asking for Confirmation during a Project Presentation.**   Work in small groups. Imagine that you and your group members have jobs developing new technology to help students learn languages. You have just invented a new product. Decide as a group what that product is, what it does, and how it works.

Examples are:

■   a TV with a mouse that allows you to click on a speaker's mouth and get an instant translation

■   an electromagnetic device that can be attached to your tongue to help you pronounce English perfectly

Next, take turns with the other groups and describe your unusual products. When you are listening, interrupt in order to clarify the descriptions of these items. When your group is speaking, be ready to answer any and all questions about *your* product.

Talk It Over

4   **Making Excuses.**   Have you ever given an excuse that was not the truth for something you forgot or did not want to do? Did the other person believe you? Or did the other person question what you said? Consider these examples:

Student: I'm sorry. I don't have my homework because my dog ate it.

Teacher: I'm not sure I understand. Do you mean to say that your dog likes to eat paper?

Woman: No, I can't go to the movies with you. I have to wash my hair.

Man: I don't get it. You mean you wash your hair every night?

Notice how the teacher challenges the student in the first example and the man challenges the woman in the second. They don't actually say the other person is lying, but it is clear that they suspect this. However, even by challenging a speaker, you may not get the truth. By asking for confirmation in a gentle tone of voice, however, you may be able to politely get the truth.

1. In pairs, practice the following pattern:

You: Make an excuse for something you don't want to do.

Your partner: Ask for confirmation, questioning the truth of the excuse.

You: Make another excuse.

Your partner: Ask for confirmation again, questioning the truth of the excuse.

Example:

Student: I'm sorry. I don't have my homework because my dog ate it.

Teacher: I'm not sure I understand. Do you mean to say that your dog likes to eat paper?

Student: Well, yes he does, actually. Some sort of vitamin deficiency, I think.

Teacher: I'm not following this. Are you telling me that paper has nutritional value?

Student: You see, when he was a puppy he was taken away from his mother too soon and…

Teacher: Wait, am I right? Do you mean to tell me that you don't have your homework because your dog had an unhappy childhood?

2. Now role-play your conversation for the class.

PART 4	# Focus on Testing

Listen to the two speakers. After each speaker finishes talking, you will hear a question. Circle the letter of the best answer to each question.

Speaker 1

a. Frank is not strong enough.

b. Frank is taking too many courses for his first semester.

c. First-year students usually take this many courses.

d. Frank has a lot of different interests.

Speaker 2

a. She is tired and hungry.

b. She doesn't want to use the meal plan on weekends.

c. She thinks the meal plan is too expensive for what she is getting.

d. She can't buy food on Sunday.

Video Activities: High-Tech Jobs and Low-Tech People

Before You Watch. Discuss these questions in small groups.

1. Which two of these are high-tech jobs?
   a. telephone repairperson
   b. computer programmer
   c. television camera operator
   d. biochemist

2. What subjects do people usually study in order to get high-tech jobs?
   a. liberal arts
   b. engineering
   c. mathematics
   d. social sciences

Watch. Circle the correct answers.

1. What is surprising about Mark Riley's work?
   a. He enjoys programming computers.
   b. He doesn't have a college degree.
   c. Programming computers used to be his hobby.

2. What problem do high-tech companies have?
   a. not enough work
   b. not enough high-paying jobs
   c. not enough qualified job applicants

3. What kind of people did high-tech companies used to look for?
   a. college graduates
   b. liberal arts graduates
   c. engineering graduates

4. According to an official at Play, Inc., what kind of people are high-tech companies looking for now?
   a. healthy
   b. smart
   c. loyal
   d. creative
   e. driven

Watch Again. Compare answers in small groups.

1. What companies are mentioned in the video?
   a. Play, Inc.   b. Manpower   c. Go High Tech

2. Which company helps people find jobs? _____

3. Complete these quotations:

   1. A job has to offer more than _____.

   2. It's not so important to Play whether or not you have a _____. It's more important that you want _____.

After You Watch. Discuss these questions with your class.

1. What are you studying? What do you plan to do when you finish studying?

2. Would you like to work in a high-tech company? Why or why not?

Chapter 3

Relationships

Did You Know?

- The longest marriage on record lasted 86 years. It was between Sir Temulji Bhicaji Nariman and Lady Nariman, who were wed in 1853 when they were five years old.

- Adam Borntrager of Medford, Wisconsin, had 675 living descendants. They were: 11 children, 115 grandchildren, 529 great-grandchildren, and 20 great-great-grandchildren.

- Compare the life expectancies for men and women in six countries:

Country	Men	Women
Japan	77.02	83.35
United States	72.5	79.87
Mexico	68.98	75.17
Russia	68.83	71.72
China	68.57	71.48

PART 1

Getting Started

Sharing Your Experience

Discuss the following questions in small groups.

1. What is life like for the elderly? Do they live with their children and grandchildren or by themselves? Do the elderly, in general, live far from or near their children? What distance do you consider far? What distance do you consider near? Use elderly family members or friends as examples in your discussion.

2. What do you know about the lifestyle of the elderly in the United States or Canada? If you know any elderly people in the United States, describe them and their daily lives. Use the questions in No. 1 to guide your discussion.

3. Where would you like to grow old? Why?

Vocabulary Preview

2 **Vocabulary in Context.** As you know, many words can have more than one meaning. The following words are some key terms used in the lecture. The definitions match the way the words are used by the speaker. Complete the following sentences with the correct forms of the vocabulary words.

assumption	*something you believe, which may or may not be true*
data	*information (which could include facts and statistics)*
disjointed	*not closely connected*
extended family	*a large number of family members living together*
household	*people living under one roof, often a family living together*
isolated	*alone; lonely*
siblings	*brothers and sisters*
statistics	*a collection of numerical data*

1. Chang had two brothers and two sisters, so there were five _____ in his family.

2. There are five people, including a grandparent, in the Smith _____.

3. The Bureau of Vital _____ keeps track of the number of marriages, births, and deaths in the United States.

4. The results of the experiment provided interesting _____; the biologist was able to use the information to solve a problem.

5. I made the _____ that you were married because you were wearing a ring on your left ring finger.

6. An _____ _____ may have children, parents, uncles, aunts, and grandparents living together.

7. Sometimes when parents divorce and the family breaks up, each family member can feel very _____.

8. When people are _____ and living alone, they may enjoy it or they may become very depressed.

3 **Using Vocabulary.** In small groups, discuss the following questions.

1. Do you have any siblings? What are their ages?
2. How many people live in your household?
3. Who is in your extended family?
4. Have you ever made assumptions that turned out to be wrong?
5. Do you think that statistics always reflect facts accurately?

PART 2

Listening for Straw Man Arguments

If you were to fight with someone made of straw, you would probably win. Thus, a "straw man" argument is an argument that can be defeated easily.

Many straw man arguments are based on assumptions, or beliefs, people have which are not true. Many professors feel that part of their job is to help students examine these beliefs that may not be true.

Therefore, instructors will often use straw man arguments in their lectures. For example, they will make a statement from one point of view (the straw man argument), and later they will demonstrate why this point of view is not accurate (defeat the argument).

Before You Listen

1   **Considering Your Assumptions.**

1.   Write brief answers to the following questions about the elderly and families. Then discuss your answers in small groups.

	In your community	In the United States
Do the elderly live with their children?		
If not, how often do the elderly see their children?		
How often do the elderly see their siblings?		
What assumptions do you think people make about the elderly?		

2.   Based on the assumptions you've made about the elderly in the United States, what straw man arguments do you think the lecturer might discuss?

Listen

2   **Listening for Straw Man Arguments.**   Listen for the straw man arguments and why they are untrue. As you listen, look at the handout on "Elderly in the United States" on page 37. Then listen again and fill in the information about some of the arguments as you listen.

Straw man argument 1: _____

_____

_____

Information the professor uses to defeat argument 1: _____

_____

_____

_____

Straw man argument 2: _____

_____

_____

Information the professor uses to defeat argument 2: _____

_____

_____

_____

Straw man argument 3: _____

_____

_____

Information the professor uses to defeat argument 3: _____

_____

_____

_____

Straw man argument 4: _____

_____

_____

Information the professor uses to defeat argument 4: _____

_____

_____

_____

After You Listen

3 **Examining Ways to Defeat Straw Man Arguments.** In small groups, discuss your answers to Activity 2.

Talk It Over

4 **Sharing Ideas Based on Assumptions.**

1. Work in small groups. Choose one of the following situations. It's all right if more than one person chooses the same situation. Also, it will be more interesting if you choose a situation that you have not experienced yet.

    What do you think it's like to:

    ■ grow old?
    ■ be a child of a single parent?
    ■ have teenage children?
    ■ live with your spouse's parents?
    ■ be married and have no children?
    ■ be married, have small children, and work?
    ■ live alone as a young person?
    ■ live alone as an old person?

2. Take two minutes to think about the situation you have chosen. What is daily life like for the person in this situation? If you have not had that experience, make guesses about that person's daily life. Then write for five minutes on the topic.

3. Share your ideas with the rest of your group. Did anyone in your group disagree with your ideas? Could anyone show that your assumptions were not accurate? How? Discuss any straw man arguments that came up as you talked.

5 **Interview: Finding Straw Man Arguments in Everyday Life.**

1. Interview someone in the community who is currently in the situation that you chose. Ask about that person's daily life. Remember to ask about some of the guesses you have made.

2. Share the results of your interview with the class. Did any of your guesses turn out to be straw man arguments? Discuss which ones, and why.

PART 3	# Making Generalizations

When we make statements about things that can be counted, we try to be accurate. For example:

> Of the 100 elderly people who were interviewed, 15 preferred to live with their children and grandchildren, 80 preferred to live alone, and 5 did not have a preference.

However, sometimes we may not know exact numbers. We cannot be accurate, but we do have some general ideas or opinions. In these cases we can describe what we think happens most of the time. We can *make generalizations*. Generalizations often contain adverbs of time.

Adverbs of Time in Generalizations

by and large	in general
for the most part	normally
generally	rarely
generally speaking	seldom
hardly ever	typically

1 Comparing Expressions.   Consider these examples:

- By and large, elderly people in the United States prefer to live alone.

   Typically, the elderly in the United States enjoy living alone.

- Rock concerts are hardly ever performed in homes for the elderly.

   For the most part, rock concerts are not performed in homes for the elderly.

- Elderly women rarely compete in races.

   Generally speaking, elderly women do not compete in races.

Work in small groups. Discuss whether the two sentences in each pair of examples have the same meaning. Tell why they do or do not have the same meaning.

2 **Listening for Generalizations.** Listen to the lecture again. Pay attention to how the instructor uses the generalizations listed in the explanation box.

1. Read the following statements. Then listen to the lecture carefully and mark the following statements T (true) or F (false) as you listen.
2. When you are finished, compare your answers with a partner.
3. In small groups, take turns changing each false statement to a true one by omitting the generalization and adding the appropriate fact.

Example of a false statement:

   F   For the most part, Americans live in large extended families.

Changed to a true statement:

   T   In the twentieth century, there was a decline in the size of American households.

1. __ Generally, people over age 65 are called elderly.

2. __ Normally, Americans move once every year.

3. __ In the United States, for the most part, marriages end in divorce.

4. __ Since Americans move a great deal, the elderly typically live far away from their children.

5. __ For the most part, the elderly in the United States prefer to live in their own homes rather than with their children.

6. __ Generally speaking, Americans live in small households.

7. __ Because of the high number of divorces and single-parent homes in the United States, the elderly rarely see their children.

8. __ Because most Americans live in small households, elderly people hardly ever see their siblings.

9. __ In general, the elderly are taken care of by family members.

10. __ By and large, the elderly frequently see their children.

Handout		Sociology Seminar 270
The Elderly in the United States		

Table 1 Elderly Living with Children or within Ten Minutes by Car: The United States and Selected European Countries

Poland	70%
Great Britain	66%
United States	61%
Denmark	52%

Table 2 Frequency of Elderly Persons' Visits with Their Children

Within 24 Hours		Last Week	
Poland	64%	Denmark	80%
Denmark	53%	United States	78%
United States	52%	Great Britain	77%
Great Britain	47%	Poland	77%

Table 3 Percentage of Elderly who Saw a Sibling within the Past Week

Women		Men	
Denmark	58%	United States	34%
United States	43%	Poland	33%
Great Britain	41%	Denmark	32%
Poland	37%	Great Britain	28%

Adapted from Ethel Shanas, "Family-Kin Networks and Aging in Cross-Cultural Perspective." *Journal of Marriage and the Family*, August 1973, pp. 508–509. Copyrighted 1973 by the National Council on Family Relations, Fairview Community School Center, 1910 West County Road B, Suite 147, Saint Paul, Minnesota 55113. Reprinted by permission.

Talk It Over

3 **Using Generalizations.** Work in groups of four. Discuss family life in your community. Think about the age when people marry, the average number of people in a household, the number of children in the average family, the divorce rate, the number of single-parent families, where the elderly live, who is responsible for earning money, and who is responsible for household chores. Use appropriate expressions for making generalizations.

PART 4   Focus on Testing

Listen to the two speakers. After each speaker finishes talking, you will hear a question. Circle the letter of the best answer to each question.

Speaker 1

a. Dad has to help Grandpa and Grandma move this week.
b. Ruth and James have to do their own homework this week.
c. Ruth and James need to practice pitching for the baseball game.
d. Ruth and James need to help around the house more than usual.

Speaker 2

a. He's explaining why he wants to take the dog along on vacation.
b. He's explaining why they have to leave the dog home this year.
c. He's trying to convince them to visit the Grand Canyon.
d. He's saying that they have to stay home to take care of the dog this summer.

Video Activities: True Love

Before You Watch.   Work in small groups. Number these causes for couples (dating or married) to end their relationship from 1 (most common) to 5 (least common).

_____ a. money problems

_____ b. different priorities

_____ c. lack of communication

_____ d. the romance is gone

_____ e. problems with family or friends

Watch.   Circle the correct answers.

1. What is Dr. Mary Quinn's job?
    a. a medical doctor
    b. a teacher
    c. a couple's counselor

2. According to the reporter, what does love not require?
    a. bonding
    b. time
    c. loyalty
    d. communication

3. What products can help couples improve their communication skills?
    a. books
    b. movies
    c. music
    d. games

4. The woman from the dating service says that after people find a partner, they often get _____.
   a. married
   b. lazy
   c. discouraged

5. Dr. Quinn says that _____ can help keep couples close.
   a. commitment
   b. marriage
   c. traditions

Watch Again.   Compare answers in small groups.

1. Check Dr. Quinn's four tips for improving communication.

   _____ a. Ask questions.

   _____ b. Choose your words carefully.

   _____ c. Listen closely.

   _____ d. Pick a good time to talk.

   _____ e. Put things in terms of yourself.

   _____ f. Make statements about your needs.

2. The woman with the red hair says that if your partner isn't thoughtful you should _____.

   a. be more thoughtful
   b. leave him/her
   c. tell him/her how you feel

3. Match the phrases with their meanings.

   1. split up   a. good feeling

   2. kick back   b. end a relationship

   3. a high   c. get lazy

After You Watch.   Discuss these questions with your class.

1. What is the divorce rate?

2. Why do you think people get divorced?

3. What do married couples do if they are having problems?

Chapter 4

Health and Leisure

Did You Know?

■ An elephant's heart rate is about 25 beats per minute. The heart rate of a canary is about 1,000 beats per minute. Most people's hearts beat about 75 times a minute. However, this rate can go to over 200 beats a minute for a short time when the body is working hard.

■ A clam's heart rate varies from 2 to 20 beats per minute. What could a clam be doing to get its heart rate up to 20 beats per minutes?

PART 1   Getting Started

Sharing Your Experience

1   The human body is often compared to a machine. For example, the eye may be compared to a camera. It automatically focuses for short and long distances and adjusts for lighting conditions. In what ways is the human body like other things? Match the parts of the body to the items. Then discuss how each body part is like the matched item.

   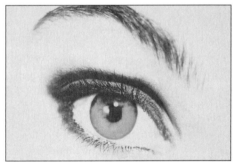

_____ 1. brain   a. scissors

__f__ 2. eye   b. computer

_____ 3. liver   c. crane

_____ 4. nervous system   d. pump

_____ 5. teeth   e. water filter

_____ 6. arm   f. camera

_____ 7. heart   g. telephone switchboard

Vocabulary Preview

2 **Vocabulary in Context.** The speakers in this chapter use the following words as they describe the heart. Complete the following sentences with the correct forms of the vocabulary words.

cardiac muscles	*muscles of the heart*
chambers	*compartments*
hollow	*having an empty space inside*
peel	*the outside covering of some fruits, such as bananas*
to pump	*to push a liquid through a system*
strip	*long, narrow piece*
tick tock	*the sound a clock makes*
to vary	*to change, differ*

1. The _____in the heart fill and empty as the heart works.

2. The_____ of the clock reminded Diana of her own heartbeat.

3. The doctor was concerned about the strength of Sue's _____ _____ after her illness.

4. The heart_____ the blood through the body.

5. Did you know that the _____contains more Vitamin C than the rest of the orange?

6. Francis used a_____ of cloth to make a bandage.

7. The size of an animal's heart _____ according to the size of the rest of its body.

8. When the doctor tapped on the patient's stomach, it sounded _____, as if there were nothing inside.

PART 2

Listening for Analogies

When instructors explain a new concept, they often compare the new idea to something that is already familiar to the students. For example, the eye may be compared to a camera. These comparisons are called *analogies*. Analogies that use *like* or *as* are called *similes*.

Expressions to Make Analogies

Expressions	*Examples*
as_____ as	The heart is as big as your fist.
(just) like	The heart works just like a pump.
similar to	The heart is similar to a clock.

Before You Listen

1   **Considering the Topic.**   Write down everything you already know about the heart. Compare your notes with those of your classmates.

_____

_____

_____

_____

Listen

2   **Listening for Analogies.**   Listen to the study session once all the way through. Then listen to the session again and write down all the analogies you hear. You can write them in short form, as in the following examples. Also note which expressions the students use to make these analogies.

Examples:
   You hear: The body is just like a machine.
   You write: <u>body = machine (just like)</u>

   You hear: The eye is similar to a camera.
   You write: <u>eye = camera (similar to)</u>

_____

_____

_____

_____

_____

_____

After You Listen

3   **Comparing Analogies.**   Share your list of analogies with your classmates. Listen to the study session again and see how many more analogies you can discover.

Talk It Over

4   **Setting Contexts for Analogies.**   In small groups, discuss the following analogies. Write down four or five situations where each analogy is appropriate. When you are finished, share your lists with the rest of the class.

Example: His hand is shaking like a leaf.

Possible situations:
He is at the dentist's office.
He is going to give a public talk for the first time.
He is trying to ask his girlfriend to marry him.
He is trying to explain to his girlfriend's father why he brought her home so late.
He just had a terrible car accident.

1. Her face is as white as a sheet.

_____

_____

_____

_____

2. He is as quiet as a mouse.

_____

_____

_____

_____

3. Her heart is pounding like a drum.

_____

_____

_____

_____

4. He is giving orders like an army general.

_____

_____

_____

_____

5. Her eyes are calm like a lake on a windless day.

_____

_____

_____

_____

5 **Discussing Analogies.**   Look at the following list of analogies. Do you know of similar expressions in other languages? Add them to the list. In small groups, discuss how these expressions may have originated. Share your results with the class.

as solid as a rock
as hard as a rock
as gentle as a lamb
as nice as pie
as happy as a clam
as white as a ghost
as quiet as a mouse
as quiet as a tomb
as free as a bird
as dumb as a post
as pretty as a picture

_____

_____

_____

_____

_____

_____

_____

PART 3 | Expressing Opinions

In the study session in this chapter, the speakers present a lot of factual information. In addition to these facts, the speakers express personal opinions. In general, when we express personal opinions, we don't want to seem like we "know it all." We want to qualify, or soften, our remarks by using specific expressions to introduce them. These expressions help the listener distinguish the facts from opinions.

Expressions to Introduce Personal Opinions

I (strongly) believe . . .   I bet . . .
I imagine . . .   I'd say . . .
I'm almost positive . . .   I'm positive . . .
I'm convinced . . .   In my opinion . . .
I'm fairly certain . . .   I suspect . . .
I'm pretty sure . . .   I think . . .
Not everyone will agree with me, but . . .

1 **Recognizing a Know-it-All.** Listen to the following conversations in which two people express their opinions. Then answer the questions.

Conversation 1

Listen to the debate between Joe and Paul.

1. Does Joe express an opinion? _____

2. Does Paul express an opinion? _____

3. Does Paul indicate that his is a personal opinion?

    _____

4. Which person sounds like a know-it-all? Why?

    _____

    _____

    _____

    _____

Conversation 2

Now listen to another version of Joe and Paul's debate.

What expressions does Paul use to introduce his personal opinions this time?

_____

_____

_____

2 **Listening for Personal Opinions.** Listen to the study session again. This time, focus on the expressions used to express opinions. Before you listen, read the following items. Each item relates to an opinion. While you listen, add the missing information to each item, using your own words if you wish.

Example: One student is convinced that the cardiac muscles are

the most amazing muscles in the human body.

1. Professor Miller is convinced that it is the action of the cardiac muscles that _____.

2. In Fred's opinion, the heart looks like _____ _____.

3. Fred imagines that the walls at the bottom of the heart are _____ _____.

4. Susan is fairly certain that _____.

5. Tory is positive that _____.

6. One student bets that scientists _____ in ten or fifteen years.

7. Fred is pretty sure that Tory's heart _____.

8. He says Tory will _____.

Talk It Over

3 **Expressing Personal Opinions.** Divide into groups of five to seven. Discuss the following three situations using appropriate expressions to introduce your personal opinions. If you wish, discuss other situations related to health.

Situation 1

The office workers in an insurance company did not do well on the yearly physical examination. They must decide what can be done to improve their physical fitness. They hold a meeting to discuss this.

Characters

- the owner of the company
- an extremely overweight accountant
- the company doctor, who smokes
- the company nurse, a vegetarian who eats healthy food
- a young executive, who jogs to work

Situation 2

Should sex education be taught in school? If so, at what age (elementary, secondary, college) and in what class (health, biology, physical education)? A school meeting is held to discuss this issue.

Characters

- a conservative parent
- a broad-minded or liberal parent
- a school principal
- a high school senior
- a counselor

Situation 3

In the United States, smoking is not allowed in classrooms, courthouses, and other public buildings. In fact, most American cities have passed laws banning smoking in places such as restaurants and shopping malls. It is banned in many workplaces, but sometimes that is a company decision. The company holds a meeting between the managers and employees to discuss this issue.

Characters

- an office worker who doesn't smoke but must work in a room with many smokers
- a student who enjoys smoking
- a pregnant woman who becomes ill from the smell of cigarette smoke
- a person with a lung disease
- an elderly person who has smoked since the age of 15

4   **Role-Play.**   In the same groups, role-play the situations from Activity 3. Stay in character as you express the opinions of the character that you are role-playing. You may add characters of your own or make up another role-play situation related to health. Choose one of the situations and perform it for the class.

PART 4   # Focus on Testing

Listen to the two speakers. After each speaker finishes talking, you will hear a question. Circle the letter of the best answer to each question.

Speaker 1

a. We should pass more laws on smoking.
b. People have a right to smoke if they want to.
c. People dying of cancer should be allowed to eat where they want to.
d. People should quit smoking at home and smoke in restaurants instead.

Speaker 2

a. She could win a bet on how much weight she can lose.
b. She is overweight, like most Americans.
c. She should lose 16 pounds.
d. Most people in America read newspapers.

Video Activities: Bottled Water

Before You Watch.   Answer and discuss these questions in small groups.

1. Where do you get your drinking water?
    a. buy it from a store   b.   from the city water supply   c.   from a well

2. Which kind of water is better in these ways? Write T for tap water or B for bottled water.
    _____ a.   price
    _____ b.   safety
    _____ c.   taste
    _____ d.   convenience

Watch.   Circle the correct answers.

1. The NRDC is probably a _____.
    a.   water bottling company   b.   consumer group   c.   doctors' organization

2. The NRDC study found that _____.
    a.   tap water is often the same as bottled water
    b.   tap water contains harmful chemicals
    c.   bottled water is safer than tap water

3. Sonia Scribner (the owner of *The Water Lady*) believes that consumers should _____.
    a.   go right to the source   b.   buy bottled water   c.   drink tap water

4. The NDRC thinks that it's time for _____.
    a.   the public to drink bottled water
    b.   the government to make tap water safer
    c.   people to realize that bottled water is not always better

Watch Again.   Compare answers in small groups.

1. What did the NRDC find in water?
    a.   lead   b.   mercury   c.   bacteria   d.   arsenic

2. Complete the statements using the numbers.

4	1/3	1,000	103	25

    a.   The public spent _____ billlion dollars on bottled water in 1997.
    b.   The NRDC tested _____ kinds of bottled water.
    c.   Some bottled water is _____ times as expensive as tap water.
    d.   The NRDC found that _____ % of bottled water is tap water.
    e.   _____ of the water tested was the same quality as tap water.

After You Watch.   Discuss the following questions with your class.

1. How careful are you about what you eat?

2. Do you buy organic fruits and vegetables?

3. Would you eat genetically altered foods? Why or why not?

Chapter 5

High Tech, Low Tech

Did You Know?

- The success of high-tech projects sometimes depends on low-tech solutions. During a space mission to close the doors on the Hubble Space Telescope, all the astronauts' high-tech repair tools failed. They finally just used their own strength to close the doors by hand.

- Astronauts F. Story Musgrave and Jeffrey Hoffman needed to replace Hubble's outdated camera with a new one. To protect the camera from damage by the sunlight, they did the job at night using only the two flashlights on their helmets and a couple more that the other astronauts shined out from the windows of the space shuttle Endeavour.

- Kathryn Thornton had to move backward as she put in COSTAR, the device used to compensate for the Hubble's defective mirror. Her coworker, Tom Akers, had to call out directions as she backed COSTAR into its parking place.

PART 1

Getting Started

Sharing Your Experience

Do the following discussion activities in small groups.

1 Divide into two groups. One person from each group should take notes. After the discussions, another person from the group should give a short report to the class.

Topic: The space program is very expensive and not everyone agrees that the government should spend so much money on this project.

Group One: You do not support funding a space program. Think of at least five other high-tech projects that might be more worthwhile than the space program.

Group Two: You do support funding a space program. List five fields of study not related to the space program that have benefited from space exploration.

2 As a class, discuss the issue of whether any country can afford to fund a space program. Consider all the time and energy that must be spent on a space program as well as the money.

Vocabulary Preview

3 **Vocabulary in Context.** The words in the following list are used in the guide's description of the simulation at the Johnson Space Center. Complete the sentences following the list with the correct forms of the vocabulary words. Note: There may be more than one correct answer.

acceleration	*the process of increasing speed*
altitude	*the distance above sea level*
astronauts	*people who fly spaceships*
atmosphere	*air surrounding the earth*
cargo bay	*an area in an airplane or spaceship used to keep cargo, special goods, or materials*
friction	*the rubbing of one thing against another; resistance to motion by two surfaces that are touching*
to manipulate	*to control*
mission	*a job*
orbit	*(n.) the circular path one body makes around another body in space (such as the moon around the earth)*
orbiter	*a vehicle or thing that orbits*
remote	*distant, far*
satellite	*an object or vehicle that orbits the earth or another body in space*
(to) shuttle	*(v.) to travel back and forth frequently; (n.) a vehicle used to shuttle*
to simulate	*to copy the appearance or effect of something*
solar	*of or about the sun*

1. _____ need a lot of training before they can be put in charge of a flight.

2. Although the scientist was on earth and the spaceship was 690 miles above earth, it was his _____ to repair the ship by _____ control.

3. In order to help the average person understand space exploration better, TV artists _____ the movement of rocket ships on the TV screen.

4. The horrified pilot found it was impossible to _____ the navigational instruments in order to steer the plane.

5. The suitcases were held in the _____ _____ of the plane.

6. As a spaceship enters the earth's _____ at an _____ of 400,000 feet, a great deal of resistance, or _____, builds up.

7. They shot up a _____ into _____ around the moon; the _____ worked perfectly.

8. There is a bus that will _____ passengers from the airport parking lot to the terminals.

9. On the outside of the spaceship you will find _____ panels, which collect the energy from the sun.

10. As the rockets fired, the _____ of the spaceship pushed the pilots into their seats.

PART 2 # Taking Notes on a Field Trip

Field trips are real-world educational experiences designed by the instructor. It is difficult to take good notes on a field trip. Often, so much information is presented that it can be confusing. Here are three hints to help you take better notes.

1. Before the field trip, get as much information as possible about the place you are going to visit. The more you already know, the easier it will be for you to understand your guide. You can read a book, look in an encyclopedia, or talk to other students who have been on a similar field trip.

2. During the field trip, write down important numbers such as measurements, years, and amounts of things. If you don't have time to write down all the information concerning the numbers, you can ask the guide or your instructor to help you fill in the missing information later.

3. After the field trip, share notes with a friend. You probably won't be able to write down every important thing, but each of you may have written down different important facts.

These three hints will help you relieve some anxiety so that you can listen well, relax, and enjoy the field trip.

Before You Listen

1 **Discussing the Handout.**   Before the space flight simulation, the guide at the Johnson Space Center hands out a diagram of the phases of the space mission. Look at the following diagram and the list of coded headings. With a partner, discuss which codes might match the pictures in the diagram.

T= Tower
OCB= Opening
    Cargo Bay
D= Deorbit
EF= Engines Fire
BR= Booster
    Rockets Drop
    Away
EO= Enter Orbit
    (altitude 690
    miles)
ET= External Tank
    Drops Away
L= Landing
RMA= Using Remote
    Manipulation
    Arm

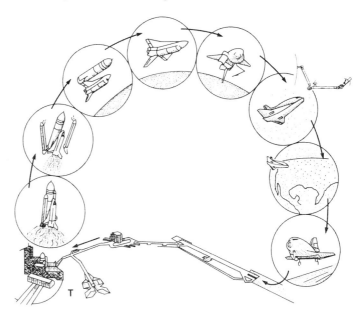

Listen

2 **Taking Notes.**

1. Listen to the simulation. As you hear about each phase of the mission in space, label each picture with the appropriate code.

2. Take notes about the Remote Manipulation Arm. Draw or write on the following diagram of the arm.

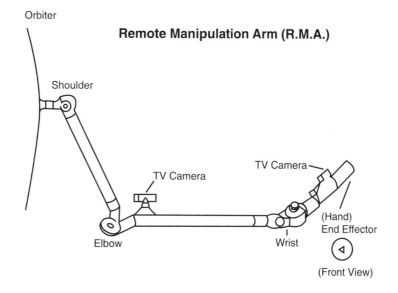

Remote Manipulation Arm (R.M.A.)

3 **Listening for Measurements and Amounts.**   Now that you have a clearer idea of the technical vocabulary used in the simulation, it will be easier to concentrate on the numbers and statistics.

1. Practice saying the following numbers aloud with a partner. Make sure you can each identify the numbers spoken.

10	=	ten
100	=	one hundred
1,000	=	one thousand
10,000	=	ten thousand
100,000	=	one hundred thousand
1,000,000	=	one million
10,000,000	=	ten million
100,000,000	=	one hundred million
1,000,000,000	=	one billion
1/2	=	one-half
1/3	=	one-third
1/4	=	one-fourth
1/10	=	one-tenth

2. Read the following items. Listen to the simulation again and complete the sentences. When you are finished, review your answers with a partner.

   1. The spaceship's acceleration builds up to _____ feet per second as we move away from the earth.

   2. The booster rockets use up their fuel and drop into the sea about _____ minutes after takeoff.

   3. As the spaceship goes into orbit, its speed is_____ times the speed of sound.

   4. When the spaceship is in orbit, it flies at an altitude of _____miles.

   5. The _____-foot mechanical arm attached to the orbiter is called the RMA.

   6. The hand, or what is called the end effector of the RMA, has _____ wires inside.

   7. The shuttle enters the earth's atmosphere at _____ feet.

   8. As the shuttle begins to deorbit, or fall to earth, it is _____ miles from its landing site.

   9. As the orbiter reaches the earth's atmosphere, its surface temperature can reach _____ degrees Fahrenheit.

   10. As the engines shut off, the orbiter continues to come down to earth at _____ feet per minute.

After You Listen

4 **Using Notes to Recall Information.**   Work in groups of three. Use your notes on the diagrams of the mission phases and the Remote Manipulation Arm to describe the phases of the mission and the use of the RMA.

Talk It Over

5 **Note Taking on Other Topics.**

1. Work with a partner. Think of a city or town that you are very familiar with and enjoy visiting. Give your partner a "mini-tour" of this city or town while he or she takes notes and asks questions. As an alternative, you may take your partner on a mini-tour of someplace other than a town – for example, a college, a factory, or a resort that you know well. Here are some kinds of information you might want to include in your tour:

    ■ points of historical interest
    ■ shopping areas
    ■ museums
    ■ city or town hall
    ■ tourist attractions, such as amusement parks, zoos, and theaters
    ■ schools and universities
    ■ geographical attractions (lakes, rivers, mountains)
    ■ systems

2. Now switch places. Listen and take notes while your partner gives you a mini-tour of his or her chosen town or place. Ask and answer questions about each other's places.

3. Present a two or three-minute report to the class about your partner's town or place.

PART 3

Shifting Between Active and Passive Voice

Using the Passive Voice

As you heard in the listening selection, instructors often use "academic English," which is impersonal and formal. To create a feeling of objectivity, they use the passive voice. Here are some hints to help you recognize the passive voice and to help you compare it with the active voice.

■ A verb in the passive voice consists of a form of the verb *to be* plus a past participle.

Example: The shuttle was flown.

■ Sometimes in sentences using the passive voice, the doer of the action is mentioned, but the doer is not as important as the subject of the sentence.

$$S \qquad V \qquad doer$$

Example: The shuttle was flown by a pilot.

Notice the use of the word "by" and the impersonal tone of the sentence.

■ In contrast, in active voice sentences the doer is the subject of the sentence and the focus of attention.

$$S = doer \; V \qquad O$$

Example: My aunt flew the shuttle.

Notice that the sentence contains a personal reference. It does not have the same neutral, impersonal tone of a passive voice sentence. In fact, in this example the speaker could even be bragging a little.

1 **Contrasting the Passive and Active Voice.** In the following four conversations, the active voice is contrasted with the passive voice, and the personal is contrasted with the impersonal. Listen to the conversations and answer the questions.

Conversation 1

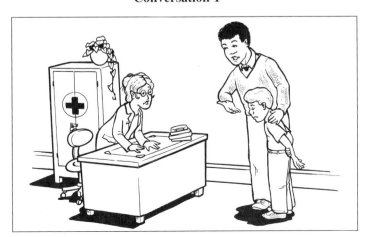

A school nurse and a teacher are talking about Mathew, a young student. Mathew is crying

Conversation 2

The school nurse is telling Mathew's father what happened.

1.   Which conversation (1 or 2) contains the passive voice? _____

2   Why do you think the passive voice was used in this situation?

_____

Conversation 3
A husband and wife are in their living room talking.

Conversation 4
A woman is on the phone with an electric company employee.

1.   Which conversation (3 or 4) contains the passive voice?

2.   Why do you think the passive voice was used in this situation?

_____

2   Listening for the Passive Voice.   Read the following incomplete sentences. Then listen for the complete sentences as you listen to the lecture for the third time. The sentences are all in the passive voice and appear in the order of their occurrence in the lecture. Complete the sentences with the correct forms of the verbs in parentheses.

1.   At T minus zero the two booster rockets fire, and three seconds later we _____ (lift) off the ground by the combined energy of the five engines.

2.   Two minutes after takeoff, the fuel in the booster rockets _____ (use up).

3.   Since the failure of its control system, the satellite has been moving through space without guidance- moving so fast that it cannot_____(reach) directly by the Remote Manipulation Arm.

4.   The hand, or what _____(call) the *end effector*, _____(fit) with three inside wires.

5.   A short arm of the satellite _____ (catch) by these wires.

6. Remember, we said that the satellite was moving too quickly _____ (pick up) directly by the RMA.

7. *Enterprise*, this is Mission Control. Congratulations! Your mission_____ (accomplish).

8. We_____ (protect) from surface temperatures of 2,750 degrees Fahrenheit by the thermal tiles covering the ship.

9. The heat is so great that radio communications _____(cut off) for 12 minutes on our descent.

Talk It Over

3 **Using the Passive Voice to Report the News.**

1. Radio and TV announcers try to remain impersonal and detached from the stories they report; therefore, the passive voice is often used in news reporting. Here are some "facts" about an imaginary accident at a space base. In small groups, take turns adding a sentence to the report, using the passive voice and the cues provided. Note that the events are in chronological order and in the past. You may add additional items.

Yesterday there was a tragic fire after a liftoff on launch pad number 2.

1. the astronauts / give
   The astronauts were given their breakfast at 5:00 A.M.

2. the countdown / begin

3. the astronauts / ask

4. the controls / check

5. all systems / test

6. the signal / give

Suddenly a fire broke out in the booster rockets before the spaceship took off.

7. the astronauts' cabin / fill

8. the fire / put out

9. the pilots / kill

10. two mechanics / injure

11. Mission Control / shock

12. burned pieces / find

13. the public / inform

14. the next mission / cancel

2. Consider an event that you have experienced or witnessed (or you may listen to a radio or TV news report and take notes). Then present this event to the class in the style of a news report. You may make this report humorous or serious. Use the passive voice to create an impersonal tone.

PART 4

Focus on Testing

Listen to the two speakers. After each speaker finishes talking, you will hear a question. Circle the letter of the best answer to each question.

Speaker 1
a.   A plane has crashed.
b.   Bad weather has closed down the airport.
c.   The pilots have refused to fly the planes.
d.   A bomb has been dropped on the airport.

Speaker 2
a.   why the space shuttle will not take off today
b.   when the repairs for the shuttle are scheduled to happen
c.   why the airport bus will not be running
d.   what kinds of repairs are needed

Video Activities: Internet Publishing

Before You Watch.

1. Match the words with their meanings.

   1. online   a. part of a story usually published in chronological order
   2. download   b. on the Internet
   3. installment c. to move information from the Internet to your computer

2. Do you use the Internet? What do you use it for?

Watch.   Circle the correct answers.

1. What kinds of things does William Bass download onto his computer?
   a. music   b. research
   c. sports articles   d. pictures

2. What is true about Stephen King's book, *The Plant*?
   a. It was published online.   b. It was free.
   c. It was published in parts. d. It was a bestseller.

3. According to William Bass, the best thing about books online is that they're _____.
   a. cheap   b. convenient   c. easy to read

4. What did Stephen King threaten to do if not enough people paid for his book?
   a. charge more for the rest of the book
   b. not write another book online
   c. not finish the rest of the book

5. Gillian McCombs says that electronic books will _____.
   a. help sell regular books
   b. let authors make more money
   c. never replace paper and ink books

Watch Again.   Compare answers in small groups.

1. How much did Stephen King charge for *The Plant*?_____

2. What was the minimum percentage of paid downloads would Stephen King accept?
   a. 25%   b. 75%   c. 95%

3. The male publishing expert says that Stephen King's book will _____.
   a. be the death of paper and ink books
   b. not change the publishing industry
   c. not be a success

After You Watch.   Discuss these questions with your class.

1. Have you ever read on a book online? If so, did you enjoy it? If not, do you think you would enjoy it?

2. Can you think of any other advantages of books online? Can you think of any disadvantages?

Chapter 6

Money Matters

Did You Know?

- In 1993 the World Bank loaned more than $18 billion to countries needing assistance with economic development.
- By 1999, the amount of money loaned to developing nations had increased to $29 billion.
- Most of the money loaned by the World Bank is used for electric power, transportation, and communication projects.
- Some people disagree with some of the projects the World Bank helps support. For example, they question the value of building a dam to provide water for crops when it leaves thousands of people homeless and destroys forests along with endangered plants and animals.

PART 1

Getting Started

Sharing Your Experience

Do the following discussion activities in small groups.

1   What are the different kinds of services that banks perform? In small groups, list as many services as you can. When you are finished, share your list with other groups in order to compile (put together) one complete list for the class.

_____

_____

_____

_____

_____

2   Are banks friends or enemies? Banks may be seen as friends in a time of need. For instance, when the owner of a small business wants to expand, he or she may go to the bank for a loan. On the other hand, banks may be seen as enemies in a time of hardship. For example, if a family is struggling to pay the mortgage on their home, the bank may foreclose and take away the property. Discuss the following questions.

1. Think of a person or family who has been helped or hurt by a bank. What did the bank do? How did this affect the people involved?
2. Can you think of a business that depends on a bank for its operation? What does the bank do for the business? Try to describe ways that the bank has helped or hurt this company.

Vocabulary Preview

3 **Crossword Puzzle.**   The following vocabulary items are from the radio program on the World Bank. Use the correct forms of the words to complete the crossword puzzle. (Answers are on page 148.)

to alleviate	*to lessen or make easier*
to borrow	*to take something with permission (with the intention of returning it)*
breeding	*mating or reproducing*
environmental	*relating to the living conditions experienced by plants, animals, and people*
insiders	*people in a group or organization who have special knowledge of its workings*
to invest	*to put money into a project in order to earn more money*
irrigation	*watering of farmland by canals, ditches, and so on*
to loan	*to give something (with the intention of getting it back)*
proposal	*a suggestion*
snail	*a simple animal in a coiled shell*
under fire	*under attack; needing defense*

Across

1. Rabbits and mice do this rapidly.
2. What you do when you need money.
3. Dry lands need this in order to produce food.
4. Sometimes money can _____ the problems of the poor.
5. Few people eat them.

Down

1. Air and water pollution problems are _____ problems.
2. You hope that the bank will _____ you money.
3. What business people often study before making decisions.
4. These people are "in the know."
5. A banker will tell you how to _____ your money.
6. She really defended her position well when she was under _____.

PART 2

Listening for Pros and Cons (Arguments For and Against)

Speakers often state arguments for and against the points they are making. These arguments are called pros and cons. To call attention to both the pro and the con arguments, a speaker uses words that indicate a switch from one point of view to the other. Read the example below.

> "Now is definitely the time to buy into this company. It's just beginning to grow and it's not well known yet, so you can buy shares at a very good price. However, there's always the chance that the company will grow too quickly and not be able to manage this growth well. In that case, you could lose some money here."

After telling why it's a good idea to invest in the company (giving a pro argument), the speaker uses the word "however" to introduce some negative information (a con argument).

Expressions Used to Change Your Point of View

although	nonetheless
but	on the contrary
however	on the other hand
instead	

Before You Listen

1 **Asking about the World Bank.**   You are going to listen to a radio program called "The World Bank under Fire." Michelle Barney, the radio station's financial reporter, interviews a guest from the World Bank and asks some very challenging questions. In small groups, list at least six questions about the World Bank.

_____

_____

_____

_____

_____

Listen

2 **Listening for Pros and Cons.**   Now listen to the radio program about the World Bank. Listen for the pros and cons of three World Bank agencies.

1. Look carefully at the following chart before you begin. Then listen to the program once all the way through.

2. Listen to the program again. This time, complete the chart as you listen. You may need to listen to the program several times to complete the chart.

Member Agencies of the World Bank		
International Bank for Reconstruction and Development	**International Development Association (IDA)**	**International Finance Corporation (IFC)**
Pros (advantages)	Pros (advantages)	Pros (advantages)
1.	1.	1.
2.	2.	2.
3.	3.	3.
Cons (disadvantages)	Cons (disadvantages)	Cons (disadvantages)
1.	1.	1.
2.	2.	2.
3.	3.	3.

After You Listen

3   **Comparing Pros and Cons.**   Compare your chart on the pros and cons of three World Bank agencies with your classmates.

Talk It Over

4   **Considering Ways to Invest Money.**   Deciding the best way to spend and invest money can be difficult. The average person tries to save some money every month, and over time these savings build up. The question is what to do with the money. Do you save it at home or do you invest it so that the amount grows? Here are some possible ways to invest money. Put this list on the board and then add your suggestions of other ways to invest money.

- Buy an apartment. Rent it now and sell it later at a profit.
- Buy individual stocks on the stock market.
- Buy mutual funds.
- Place your money into a bank account that pays above-average interest.
- Buy 1,000 lottery tickets.
- _____
- _____
- _____
- _____
- _____

$$$
Guaranteed Rates
for the
Serious Investor

INVESTMENT CERTIFICATES

$10,000 "Mini Jumbo"

TERM	RATE	YIELD
3 MONTHS	3.25	3.29
6 MONTHS	3.60	3.67
12 MONTHS	3.92	4.00

$100,000 "Giant Jumbo"

TERM	RATE	YIELD
3 MONTHS	3.35	3.39
6 MONTHS	3.60	3.67
12 MONTHS	3.95	4.03

$10,000 minimum investment on "Mini Jumbo" and $100,000 minimum investment on "Giant Jumbo." Penalty for early withdrawl. Available to California residents only.
Interest paid monthly or deposited to passbook account.
(LIMITED OFFER)

FIRESIDE *Thrift*

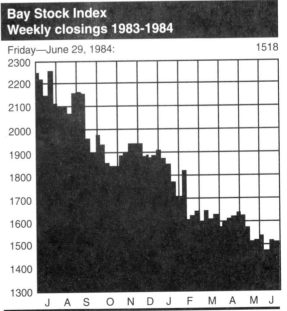

Source: Merrill Lynch

5 **Discussing Pros and Cons of Investments.** Work in small groups. Discuss the pros and cons of the investments listed on the board.

1. List as many pros and cons as the group can think of for each type of investment.
2. Examine your group's list of pros and cons carefully. Then take a vote on which investment your group thinks is the best.
3. Report the results of the voting to the rest of the class.

PART 3 # Agreeing and Disagreeing

Often in schools, colleges, and universities in the United States and other English-speaking countries, when instructors give a point of view, they expect students to react to their statements by agreeing or disagreeing. Expressing your own point of view is valued as independent thinking. Of course, being able to agree or disagree is valuable outside, as well as inside, the classroom. Every day most of us are asked to give our points of view in conversations with friends, relatives, and acquaintances.

To feel comfortable when we make a point, we need to know the vocabulary of agreeing and disagreeing. We also need to know which expressions are polite and which are not.

Expressions for Expressing Agreement

Informal	*Formal*
Absolutely!	Exactly. (Exactly right.)
I'll say!	I agree.
I knew it!	I agree with that.
That's/You're right.	I couldn't agree more.
That's for sure!	That's (absolutely) true.
You'd better believe it!	That's/You're correct.
You can say that again!	That's precisely the point.

Expressions for Expressing Disagreement

Informal	*Formal (assertive)*
That's a laugh!	I don't agree.
That's a joke!	I don't believe that.
You don't know what you're talking about!	I don't think so at all.
	I'm afraid not.
You've got to be joking !	No, definitely not.
You've got to be kidding!	You couldn't be more wrong.

Formal (polite)

I guess that's true, but . . .
I guess you could say that, but. . .
I understand what you mean, but . . .
That's more or less true, but . . .
Yes, but isn't it also true that . . .

1   **Listening for Appropriate Uses of Expressions.**   Listen to the following conversations in which expressions of agreement and disagreement are used both appropriately and inappropriately. Then answer the questions.

Conversation 1

In a college classroom, a student is challenging an instructor.

1.   Do you think the student is being polite or rude? _____

2.   Why? _____

Conversation 2

Now listen to a different student respond to the same instructor.

1. Do you think this student responded appropriately?_____

2. Why or why not? _____

Conversation 3

Two students are chatting in the school cafeteria.

Paul probably doesn't have too many friends. Why do you think this might be?

_____

Conversation 4

Let's give Paul another chance to respond to Roger a bit more appropriately.

Why is the expression that Paul uses this time to agree with Roger more appropriate?

_____

Conversation 5

At a corporation meeting, two board members are discussing future plans.

1.   Do you think these board members will reach an agreement easily? _____

2.   Why or why not? _____

Conversation 6

Now listen to two other board members in a similar conversation.

1.   How is this conversation different from the previous one?

_____

2.   Do you think these board members will be able to reach an agreement more or less easily than the board members in the previous conversation?

_____

Conversation 7

At the doctor's office, a doctor is discussing her patient, a 12-year-old boy, with his mother.

1.   Is Mrs. Franklin, the boy's mother, agreeing or disagreeing with the doctor? ____

2.   Is Mrs. Franklin responding formally or informally? _____

Conversation 8

Listen to the doctor and Mrs. Franklin again. This time Mrs. Franklin responds differently.

1. Is Mrs. Franklin responding formally or informally? _____

2. Which of the two responses do you think is more appropriate? Why? _____

_____

2   **Agreeing and Disagreeing.**   Listen to the radio program again. This time your instructor will stop the tape or CD ten times so that you can practice using appropriate expressions to agree or disagree with the speaker. Use the list of expressions from the explanation box. When you agree with a point, support your idea with an example from your own experience. When you disagree, give your reason.

Before listening, read the following sentences. They will be the last sentences you hear before your instructor stops the tape, so it is important that you understand them.

Stop 1   *But it turns out that money isn't everything.*

Stop 2   *The critics of the World Bank say that this kind of help to developing countries is wasteful, destructive, and unfair.*

Stop 3   *Isn't it also true that this just means that developing countries are forced to cut spending on health, education, transportation, and welfare programs in order to reduce their huge debts to the World Bank?*

Stop 4   *Well, this rule is good for the countries and companies that want to sell goods to developing countries, but wouldn't this discourage local production of goods?*

Stop 5   *...we know that technological advances can sometimes cause environmental problems...*

Stop 6   *...understanding local needs and culture may be more important than anything else in the success of a project.*

Stop 7   *So this is how contributing nations can dictate what governmental policies must be in place before loans will be given, right?*

Stop 8   *This is good for the country because the government does not have to guarantee the loan and it encourages the growth of private business and industry.*

Stop 9   *...the loan is more effective if people in the region spend the money in ways they think are best...*

Stop 10   *We all know that it is difficult to separate economic goals from political interests in today's world.*

3 **Discussing Current Events.** Practice expressions for agreeing and disagreeing while discussing current events.

1. Find a newspaper or magazine article that you feel strongly about and bring a copy to class.
2. Summarize the major issue in the article for the class.
3. State the author's point of view and explain why you agree or disagree. Use the stronger, less polite forms of disagreement. However, be aware that the expressions you use often say more about you than about the topic you are discussing.

Talk It Over

4 **Simulation.**   In this activity you will come up with a plan to help a country called "Potential Prosperity."

1. As a whole class, read the following information about the struggling country of Potential Prosperity.
2. Work in groups of five or six. Each group should come up with at least five actions that could be taken to improve the economic conditions in Potential Prosperity.
3. Take turns reporting your group's suggestions for action.
4. When a suggestion is made by another group, the members of your group should say whether they agree or disagree with the suggestion and why.

Be sure to use the expressions of agreement and disagreement presented in this chapter. Begin with formal expressions; then, as the discussion continues, use the stronger, less polite expressions if you wish.

The Land of Potential Prosperity

    abundant natural resources (recently discovered): oil, uranium
    a common language (spoken by all)
    several large towns
    several large rivers flowing from the mountains
    a large lake
    a pleasant climate
    a mountainous central region
    landlocked (no outlet to the sea)
    only one major export
    imports greatly exceed exports
    high unemployment rate
    high illiteracy rate
    high inflation rate
    poor soil
    a large population
    a low hourly wage
    unfriendly neighbors

PART 4

Focus on Testing

Listen to the two speakers. After each speaker finishes talking, you will hear a question. Circle the letter of the best answer to each question.

Speaker 1
a.   Banks are loaning less money to people with low incomes than in the past.
b.   There are pros and cons to accepting bank loans.
c.   The bank gives away money to the poor.
d.   Banks use string to tie up sacks of money.

Speaker 2
a.   I didn't understand what you said.
b.   I don't agree with you.
c.   It can take years to save enough money to buy something.
d.   You will save money if you pay cash for something.

Video Activities: Welfare Payments

Before You Watch.   Discuss these questions in small groups.

1. What kinds of problems do you think that the Department of Social Services (DSS) takes care of?

   a.   health   b.   poverty   c.   traffic   d.   tax

2. A grand jury listens to evidence and decides _____.

   a.   if a person is guilty or innocent
   b.   on appropriate punishment for a criminal
   c.   whether a crime has been committed

3. What kind of crime is graft?

Watch.   Circle the correct answers.

1. What was the grand jury's decision about DSS?

   a.   They weren't giving poor families enough help.
   b.   They often gave money to people that shouldn't get it.
   c.   They needed a new director.

2. The grand jury felt that DSS's slogan <u>should</u> be, "When in doubt, _____ it out."

   a.   check   b.   give   c.   put

3. What does the DSS's slogan in Question #2 mean?

   a.   If you aren't sure about whether to give people money or not, get more information.
   b.   If you don't know who should get help, ask your supervisor.
   c.   If you have facts about a case, tell the people in charge.

4. What is Jake Jacobson's job?

   a.   a lawyer for DSS   b.   a client of DSS   c.   director of DSS

5. The grand jury _____ Jacobson.

   a.   praised   b.   criticized   c.   fired

Watch Again.   Complete the statements using the numbers.

20-30	7	20	60

1. DSS gives out $_____ million in overpayments a year.

2. The county board of supervisors will have _____ days to study the report.

3. The grand jury said that nothing had changed at DSS for the past ____ years.

4. The report said that _____ % of the DSS payments were fraudulent.

After You Watch.   Discuss these questions in small groups.

1. How do poor families get help in your community?

2. Do you think that the government should help poor families? If not, why not? If so, what kinds of help should they get?

Chapter 7

Remarkable Individuals

Did You Know?

- In 1907 Alphonse Steines was looking for a good location for a bicycle race. While driving in the Pyrenees Mountains in France he was forced to leave his car in the heavy snow and struggle on foot for 12 km over the mountains to a police station on the other side. The next morning, perhaps to play a joke on his friend Henri Desgrange, the originator of the Tour de France bicycle race, Steines telegrammed: "I have crossed the mountains on foot at night. The roads are passable for vehicles. No snow."

- Perhaps not knowing how difficult it would be, Henri Desgrange organized the first Tour de France bicycle race in 1910 in the Pyrenees Mountains. The remarkable first racers were required to carry all their own food, clothing, and spare parts with them on their one-speed bikes. Many of the racers did not finish the race.

- The first time an American won the Tour de France bicycle race with an American team and an American bicycle was in 1999. This racer was Lance Armstrong. The only other American winner, Greg Lamond, was riding for a European team on a European bicycle when he won several times—in 1986, 1989, and 1990. Lance Armstong won again in 2000 and 2001.

PART 1   # Getting Started

Sharing Your Experience

1   Discuss the following in small groups.

1. Who are some of the most remarkable people around the world? What have they done? What do they have in common?
2. Who are the some of the most remarkable people you know personally? What have they done? What do they have in common?
3. What do you think is the most remarkable thing you have ever done? Remember: you don't have to be famous to be remarkable. Sometimes the things we accomplish every day are extraordinary.

Vocabulary Preview

2 **Definitions.** You will hear these words in the celebrity profile. Before you listen, work with a partner to write the letter of the correct definition beside each word.

_____ 1. to battle	a. the most important or best part
_____ 2. bull	b. to fight
_____ 3. chemotherapy	c. a section of the spine or backbone
_____ 4. to endure	d. to stay equal with
_____ 5. fluke	e. a male animal of some species that is strong and aggressive and mates with many females
_____ 6. from scratch	f. an accident; a lucky surprise
_____ 7. highlight	g. lacks self-discipline; does not follow rules
_____ 8. to hit-and-run	h. from the beginning, starting with nothing
_____ 9. to keep up with	i. to experience success
_____ 10. to ride high	j. to have an accident and run away without helping or reporting it
_____ 11. undisciplined	k. to go through something very difficult
_____ 12. vertebra	l. a medical treatment for cancer

3 **Using Vocabulary.** Discuss your answers to the following questions with a partner.

1. Describe an issue that you have battled. (For example, some students are <u>undisciplined</u> and must <u>battle</u> poor study habits or they cannot keep up with the other students). Did you succeed?
2. Describe the qualities of a <u>bull</u>.
3. Have you or anyone you know ever <u>endured</u> a difficult situation? Describe it.
4. These days it is remarkable to be able to cook anything <u>from scratch</u>. What can you (or your friends or family) make from scratch?
5. What has been the <u>highlight</u> of your year so far? Are you still <u>riding high</u> on it?
6. How many <u>vertebrae</u> do you have? Count them.

PART 2 # Listening for Chronological Order

Chronological order is a method of organization based on time. Simple chronological order begins with the earliest event and ends with the most recent event. History is often presented in simple chronological order. Most lectures, however, are usually more than just a presentation of facts in chronological order. For example, in order to compare recent events with those of the past, the speaker moves forward and backward in time.

Note the following expressions that indicate time or sequence. They will help you follow the actual sequence of events, even if a speaker does not use chronological order.

Time and Sequence Words

_____ after	_____ later
_____ afterward	_____ long ago
_____ at that time	_____ next
_____ before	_____ now
_____ by ... (time)	_____ past
_____ during	_____ present
_____ eventually	_____ present day
_____ finally	_____ presently
_____ first	_____ recently
_____ formerly	_____ soon
_____ from ... to. . .	_____ then
_____ in ... (date)	_____ today
_____ in ... (adjective) times	_____ until
_____ last	_____ while

In addition to listening for time and sequence words, it is also important to follow the logic of the facts being presented. Use the following clues to help you understand the time sequence of events, or chronological order.

- common sense
- word repetition
- the use of pronouns to refer to previously mentioned nouns
- the choice of definite and indefinite articles ("the" versus "a")

Before You Listen

1 **Putting Events in Chronological Order.**   Work in small groups. Read the three sentences aloud. Then use the clues above to help you answer the questions.

1. By dinnertime he still had not returned.
2. Kristen was waiting for her husband to return from his training ride.
3. Eventually, she phoned his coach to find out what had happened to him.

Which of the sentences should be first? _____

Why? _____

Which should come second? _____

Why? _____

Which is third?   _____

Why? _____

Listen

2 **Listening for Time and Sequence Expressions.**   Listen to the celebrity profile once all the way through. Each time you hear one of the time expressions from the explanation box, make a check mark beside it.

3 **Organizing Information in Chronological Order.**   Read the statements on the following chart. Listen to the celebrity profile again. As you listen, put an "X" in the box for the correct time frame for each statement.

Statements	During Armstrong's youth	Before he found out that he had cancer	After he found out that he had cancer	In the future
1. Armstrong won the Tour de France.			×	
2. He became an international cycling champion.				
3. He was called the "Bull from Texas."				
4. He was poor.				
5. He built up a lot of heavy muscle.				
6. He built strong and light muscles.				
7. He had a son.				
8. He was hit by a car.				
9. He wants to cross the finish line while his wife and ten children applaud.				
10. He wants to lie in a field of sunflowers.				

After You Listen

4   **Comparing Your Answers.**   In small groups, compare your charts. Discuss how you determined the time frame for each item.

5   **Completing a Timeline.**   With a partner, use your chart and other information you remember from the celebrity profile to complete the timeline of Lance Armstrong's life. Can you think of any other events to add to the timeline?

Lance Armstrong's Life

He lived in Plano, Texas.	1980's
He was poor.	
_____	1990
He was called the "Bull from Texas."	1991—1996
_____	1996
He found out that he had cancer.	_____
_____	1997
He won the Tour de France.	1999
His son Luke was born.	_____
_____	2000
He was selected for the U.S. Olympic team.	_____
_____	2000
He won a bronze medal.	_____
_____	2001

Talk It Over

6   **Telling a Story.**   Work in small groups in a circle. Use the following story starters as the first line of a story. The first student reads the sentence and continues the story by adding another sentence. The second student adds another sentence to the story, the third student adds another one, and so on. Continue in this manner until every student has had at least two turns before you end each story. As you are making up each story, look back at the list of time and sequence words on page 78 and use as many of them as you can. If possible, tape-record your stories and play them back to the class.

Story Starters

1. Since this was the first day off that Janna had had in over a week, she intended to put her feet up and enjoy a good book. But that isn't what happened! What happened was . . .

2. Harry hated flying. In fact, you could say that he was a complete coward unless his feet were firmly planted on the ground. But when the engine caught fire . . .

3. When Shadia was born she looked quite ordinary. There didn't seem to be anything special about her at all. But when she was about two years old . . .

PART 3 # Expressing Likes and Dislikes

There are a great variety of expressions for likes and dislikes. The type of situation (whether it's formal or informal, for example) must be considered before choosing which expression to use.

The following expressions are some of the most common ones for expressing likes and dislikes. They are listed in order from the gentlest to the strongest. In formal situations, the strongest expressions of dislike are probably not appropriate. And even in very informal situations, in order to be considerate of someone's feelings, you might also use one of the gentler expressions of dislike when expressing your opinion.

In addition, when choosing between making a gentle or a strong statement, you should also consider your tone of voice. Tone of voice is often more important than the actual expression you choose. Anger or sarcasm in your voice, for example, cannot hide behind the gentlest of expressions.

Expressing Likes		**Expressing Dislikes**	
gentlest	I like . . .	**gentlest**	I don't especially like . . .
	I enjoy. . .		I don't care for . . .
	I'm pleased.		I dislike . . .
	I'm happy.		I don't have time for . .
	I appreciate. . .		I can't tolerate . . .
	I'm delighted.		. . .irks me/bugs me. (informal)
	I'm thrilled.		
	This is my idea of. . .		. . .is more than I can stand.
	That's terrific/great/super!		I can't take/stand/bear . . .
	What a terrific/great/ super. . .!		What a rotten . . .
			I hate . . .
strongest	I love . . .	**strongest**	I detest . . .

1   **Listening for Appropriate Expressions.**   Listen for the expressions of likes and dislikes in the following conversations. Then answer the questions.

Conversation 1

A man is being interviewed for a job.

1.   Do you think the man will get the job? _____

2.   Why or why not? _____

_____

_____

Conversation 2

A woman is being interviewed for a job.

1.   Do you think the woman will get the job? _____

2.   Why or why not? _____

_____

_____

_____

Conversation 3

Rafael and Ana are discussing what to do with their leisure time.

1.   Does Ana enjoy concerts? _____

2.   Does she express her opinion strongly, or does she soften it? _____

3.   Do you think Rafael will ask Ana out again? Why or why not? _____

_____

_____

Conversation 4

Rafael and Joyce are discussing what to do with their leisure time.

1.   Does Joyce enjoy experimental theater? _____

2.   Does she express her opinion strongly? _____

3.   Do you think Rafael will ask Joyce out again? Why or why not? _____

_____

_____

2 **Listening for Expressions of Likes and Dislikes.** At several points in the lecture on Lance Armstrong, the speaker expresses a like or a dislike of his or someone else's. Listen to the lecture again. This time, write down all the expressions of likes and dislikes that you hear. When you are finished, compare your answers with those of your classmates.

_____

_____

_____

_____

_____

_____

3 **Choosing Appropriate Expressions.** Work in small groups. For each of the following situations, decide what to say to the person you meet and to the friend who is with you. Choose an appropriate expression and tone of voice. Share your responses with the group.

1. A man is sitting in front of you at the movie theater with his three noisy children. They are throwing popcorn at each other and talking too much. They are nothing like your three remarkable children. You have already asked the father politely to do something about the situation, but there has been no change. It's time to take stronger action.

To the father: _I would really appreciate it if you would quiet down your children._

To your friend: _Let's move; I can't stand this._

2. You are at a nightclub with your friends. Someone keeps asking you to dance. You have already refused twice, but this person will not take no for an answer.

To the person: _____

To your friends: _____

3. Your favorite restaurant is not as good as it used to be. Now the restaurant is not clean, the waiters are rude, and the food is often of poor quality. You and a friend have decided to give the restaurant one last chance, and as you are eating a terrible soup, the owner approaches you and asks you if everything is all right.

To the owner: _____

To your friend: _____

4. You and a friend have enrolled in a course on public relations. Unfortunately, the instructor often changes the subject and tells long and uninteresting stories about his travel adventures. You want to spend your time learning more about public relations.

To the instructor: _____

To your friend: _____

Talk It Over

4 **Discussing Goals and Interests.**

1. Look at the following chart of remarkable goals and interests. Circle those things that you would really enjoy doing and make an X through the ones you would not like to do.

2. Add other goals or interests in the blank boxes.

3. In small groups, discuss why you marked your charts the way you did. Use expressions on page 81 to express your likes and dislikes.

Arts	Sports	Home	Career	Relationships	Adventure	Other
become an artist	ride a bicycle around the world	build a house from scratch	start an Internet company	date a movie star	Climb Mt. Everest	
take news photos	go bungee jumping	live on a houseboat	win the Nobel Prize for chemistry	have more than one husband or wife	travel to Antarctica	
play in a famous rock band	kick the winning goal at the World Cup Soccer Finals	have homes in New York, Paris, Tokyo, and Hong Kong	be a fashion model	have a relationship someone you meet on the Internet	ride in a hot air balloon	
sing at the opera	win an Olympic gold medal in gymnastics	live on a space station	own your own business	make friends with someone from another country	sail around the world	

PART 4 **Focus on Testing**

Listen to the two speakers. After each speaker finishes talking, you will hear a question. Circle the letter of the best answer to each question.

Speaker 1

a. Garage sales are a waste of time.
b. Looking at famous people is ridiculous.
c. Sunday is the best day of the week.
d. Sunday is a good day for a garage sale.

Speaker 2

a. Reading is a great class.
b. A class to study the biographies of remarkable people is a good idea.
c. Every class should have a book list.
d. All remarkable people should write their autobiographies.

Video Activities: Overcoming Serious Illness

Before You Watch.   Discuss these questions in small groups.

1. When you are paralyzed, _____.
   a.   you cannot move some muscles
   b.   you are in a lot of pain
   c.   your bones are broken

2. A stroke affects your _____.
   a.   heart
   b.   brain
   c.   lungs

Watch.   Circle the correct answers.

1. Brian Davis became paralyzed when he had _____.
   a.   an accident
   b.   a stroke
   c.   a heart attack

2. What part of Brian Davis's body was paralyzed?
   a.   his arms
   b.   his left leg
   c.   his right side

3. What did Brian Davis have to relearn?
   a. walking
   b. thinking
   c. talking
   d. swallowing

4. What part of Brian Davis's body is still paralyzed?
   a. one arm
   b. one leg
   c. one hand

5. Who promised to ride with Brian?
   a. his brother
   b. his friend
   c. his doctor

6. Circle the adjectives that describe Brian.

determined	depressed	courageous
weak	hardworking	content

Watch Again.   Compare answers in small groups.

1. How long ago was Brian's accident?
   a. 1 year
   b. 6 months
   c. 5 years

2. What is Brian's advice to people in his situation?

3. What is Brian's next challenge?
   a. to climb a mountain
   b. to become a doctor
   c. to ride without training wheels

After You Watch.   Discuss these questions with your class.

1. Have you ever known anyone who recovered from a serious illness or accident? Tell the class their story.

2. What lesson can we all learn from Brian Davis's story?

Chapter 8

Creativity

Did You Know?

- Grandma Moses (Anna Mary Robertson Moses) lived on a farm all her life and never had a single art lesson. However, when she was over 70 years old, she began to paint and soon became a widely known and very successful artist.

- Wolfgang Amadeus Mozart was regarded as a creative genius by the time he was five years old. His ability to compose and perform music was far greater than that of most well-trained adult musicians of his time.

- R. Buckminster Fuller was an architect and inventor who came up with ways of getting the most use out of the least amount of material. He is best known for the geodesic dome, an inexpensive style of building that can be used for homes, workshops, barns, or storage.

PART 1

Getting Started

Sharing Your Experience

Being creative is not limited to scientists or artists. There are a multitude of amateur inventors who keep finding new and more convenient ways of doing everyday things. For example, the paper clip was invented by a man who kept losing his paperwork. In addition to becoming a millionaire, he became very well organized! Do the following discussion activities in small groups.

1   Discuss the following list of inventions and describe how they are creative solutions to everyday problems. In your discussion, you might consider the things they replaced.

- lightbulb
- washing machine
- ballpoint pen
- refrigerator
- rubber band
- Post-it or "sticky" note
- Velcro

2 Often we are unable to see the potential uses for familiar objects. In small groups, closely look at an ordinary object such as a rubber band, a ballpoint pen, or a safety pin. Brainstorm a list of ten things you could do with the object (aside from its normal use, of course). Share your list with the whole class.

3 Sit in a circle if possible. Take any ordinary object you see around you: a cup, a leaf, a pencil, a sweater. Give the object you have to the person on your left, and take the object from the person on your right. Now, let your thoughts flow as freely as you can about how the object you are now holding represents your personality (or the personality of someone you know or someone famous). Try to think of at least five examples and share these with the group. For instance:

A leaf . . .
- can be very fragile and so am I at times.
- can be very strong and so am I at times.
- goes through many changes in its lifetime and so do I.
- is flexible and bends easily and most of the time I do too.
- just hangs around and I like to do that too.

Vocabulary Preview

4 **Vocabulary in Context.** The following words from the lecture relate to key aspects of the topic of creativity. Complete the following sentences with the correct forms of the vocabulary words.

analytical	*examines closely, considering all details*
to circumnavigate	*to go completely around something*
fragmentary	*broken into parts*
to fuse	*to bind together*
to inhibit	*to block or frustrate*
original	*unique, the first one of its kind*
solution	*an answer to a problem*
to specialize	*to limit to a very narrow area of use or study*

1. If you have a very _____ mind, you will tend to examine both objects and issues very closely.

2. Ferdinand Magellan was the first man to _____ the earth.

3. Even though I had practiced the speech for many weeks, as soon as I saw the huge audience, I became _____ and couldn't say anything at all.

4. Intense heat may _____ the nuclei of two atoms.

5. He couldn't find a _____ to the problem because his knowledge of the subject was incomplete and _____.

6. If you _____ too much in any field of knowledge, you may lose sight of its relation to other aspects of life.

7. To develop your own identity, you can't always imitate others; you have to be _____.

Listening for Signal Words

In speaking and writing, we often use signal words to prepare our audience for what is to come, what our next idea will be. This allows the audience to listen more effectively. Listening for signal words is especially important when attending a lecture because it helps us take notes. If an instructor says, "Now I'm going to outline today's subject for you," we know to prepare ourselves to do outlining. If the instructor says, "Now I'm going to review yesterday's material," we know to think about the topic covered the day before and perhaps to look back over our notes. Signal words prepare us for what is going to happen next and what we need to do in response.

Verbs That Serve as Signal Words

____analyze	____ emphasize	____ list
____answer	____ evaluate	____ outline
____consider	____ explain	____ pick up (where we left off)
____continue	____ go on (with)	____ repeat
____define	____ go over	____ review
____describe	____ illustrate	____ summarize
____discuss		

Before You Listen

1 **Thinking about Creativity.**   Think about the following questions. Share your thoughts in small groups.

1. Do you think of yourself as a very creative person, a little creative, or not creative at all? Give reasons for your answer.

2. Do you like to play word games and solve puzzles, or do you avoid these activities? What makes them fun or not fun for you?

3. Are you a serious or a playful person? In what ways?

4. Do you think that a person who is logical can be creative? Why or why not?

5. Do you think people who like things to stay the same are likely to be creative? What about people who like change? Are they likely to be creative?

Listen

2   **Listening for Signal Words.**

1.   First, listen to the lecture once all the way through to get the main ideas. As you listen, list the blocks to creativity that the lecturer describes.

_____

_____

_____

_____

_____

_____

_____

_____

George Seurat used dots of color to create his painting *Afternoon on the Island of La Grande Jatte.*

```
┌─────────────────────────────┐
│         HANDOUT             │
│  ─────────────────────────  │
│                             │
│       ●    ●    ●           │
│                             │
│       ●    ●    ●           │
│                             │
│       ●    ●    ●           │
│                             │
│         Dot puzzle          │
└─────────────────────────────┘
```

2.   Listen to the lecture again. This time, listen for the signal words from the explanation box. Every time you hear one of these words or phrases, put a check mark next to it. Listen until you have found at least six signal words.

3.   Listen to the lecture a third time. This time pay particular attention to what happens *after* each signal word or phrase. Write the signal word or phrase in the following chart and note what the speaker does after each signal word. (Hint: If the lecturer has used the signal word effectively, your answer will include a definition or synonym for this word.)

Signal words	What comes next; what the lecturer does
1. continue	goes on with the discussion of the creative process
2. pick up where we left off	begins with the idea started at the end of the last class

After You Listen

3 **Comparing Notes.**   Work with a partner.

1. Compare your notes from Activity 2. Did you list the same blocks to creativity and signal words?
2. Share which blocks fit you and which do not. Explain why.

Talk It Over

4 **Using Your Creativity.**   If you were placed in a cell with another person and not allowed to speak or write, what methods would you devise to communicate with the other person? Share your responses in small groups.

5 **Using Signals.**   Human beings use more than language to signal each other. Two signals that people use—often unconsciously—are tone of voice and body language. Tone of voice and body language tell us how people really feel despite their words. As people's moods and intentions change, their voices and bodies reflect those changes. If you are alert, you can read the deeper meanings of the words people say by noticing the tone they use and their posture, gestures, and other body language.

1. To get a feeling for using tone of voice and body language as you communicate, push back the desks and stand in a circle with your classmates and instructor.
2. Take turns saying an insignificant sentence to someone across the room from you. Take a few steps as you say the sentence to get your whole body into the act, not just your face and voice. Use this sentence, or make up your own if you prefer.

Apples are red and bananas are yellow.

3. Your instructor or a classmate will suggest an adjective to describe your attitude as you say the sentence. Here are a few adjectives to get you started. Add as many as you can to this list.

angry	frightened	murderous
delighted	frustrated	rushed
disgusted	grieving	sarcastic
flirtatious	inhibited	shy

6 **Researching the Topic.** We have been discussing one way signaling occurs in language. But other kinds of signaling go on all the time among human beings, animals, insects, plants, and even individual cells. For example, cells send chemical messages to one another; plants use pollen, scent, and insects to send messages; birds use markings, like the color of their feathers, and sound. Below are the names of some animals and insects that are well known for their ability to signal and communicate:

whales	ants	monkeys	mockingbirds	skunks
bees	dogs	dolphins	cockroaches	

1. Form small discussion groups. Each person should choose one of the animals or insects listed (or any other you know about).

2. Research to find out how it signals and communicates. Make notes to use for a brief lecture on this topic.

3. Meet with your groups again. Take turns describing the major ways each animal or insect communicates. Use signal words in your talk to prepare your classmates for what will come next.

4. Discuss these questions after everyone in your group has had a chance to present.
   ■ How do these animal forms of communication compare to human communication?
   ■ Are they as creative?

PART 3   # Divulging Information

To divulge means "to give out or disclose." In colloquial English, if someone is divulging information, the implication is that we are being told something important that everyone may not know—"the inside information," "what is really happening."

Information that is *divulged* is a different quality from other information given during a conversation or a lecture. It is important in note taking and outlining that you recognize when information is being divulged because it might be this information that you will be expected to take most seriously and that you will probably be tested on. When a lecturer is about to divulge something, he or she usually announces this intention.

Expressions for Divulging Information

Despite what you may believe . . .
Despite what you may have heard . . .
Here's how it really is.
The fact of the matter is . . .
The reality is that . . .
What's really going on here is . . .

Slang Expressions for Divulging Information in Informal Situations

The (real) deal is . . .
The real scoop is . . .
The real story is . . .
What really gives is . . .
Where it's really at is . . .

1 **Listening for Ways of Divulging Information.**   Listen to these conversations that present examples of ways to divulge information.

Conversation 1

Albert and Bonnie are discussing the real reason that Professor Stone was fired. Listen to the speakers and answer the questions.

1. Is this conversation formal or informal? _____

2. What phrase helped you decide this? _____

Conversation 2

Kate and Doug are discussing where Jules got the money for his new motorcycle. Listen to the speakers and answer the questions.

1. Is this conversation formal or informal? _____

2. What phrase helped you decide this? _____

2 **Listening for Information That Is Divulged.**

1. Listen to the lecture again. Pick out the phrases that signal that information is about to be divulged. Write them down in the following chart. Listen also for the specific information that is divulged. Take notes on this information in the chart also.

Victor Varsarely inventively used curved lines and bars of black and white to create *Tampico*.

Phrases the lecturer uses to divulge information	Information divulged
1.	
2.	
3.	
4.	
5.	

2. Discuss the following questions with your classmates. Is the information that the lecturer divulges in this way critical to the main points of the lecture? Why or why not?

Talk It Over

3 **Completing Conversations.**

1. Look at the following incomplete conversations. With a partner, complete as many of the conversations as you can in the time you are given. Use as many of the expressions for divulging information as you can.

2. Choose one conversation and role-play it for the class.

    1.   A: What's up? I hear Frank's moving to Toledo.

       B: Nah, _____

       A: _____

       B: _____

    2.   A: I don't understand this at all. Helen tells me one thing and Jean tells me another. What's going on?

       B: _____

       A: _____

       B: _____

    3.   A: I just saw Alan and he looked pretty upset. What's the story? He said he was just a little tired, but he looked really worried to me.

       B: _____

       A: _____

       B: _____

    4.   A: Hey, what gives? I thought you'd gotten an A in that class. Paul says that you impressed everyone with your last creative writing project.

       B: _____

       A: _____

       B: _____

    5.   A: Where do you think I should exhibit my paintings? Henry suggested the gallery over by the museum, but Vicki said that not many people go there.

       B: _____

       A: _____

       B: _____

6. A: Hey, I thought this was supposed to be a surprise party! If we arrive at 6:00, won't he already be there? What's the scoop?

    B: _____

    A: _____

    B: _____

Focus on Testing

Listen to the two speakers. After each speaker finishes talking, you will hear a question. Circle the letter of the best answer to each question.

Speaker 1
a. There's a picture by Grandma Moses in the gallery.
b. Artists should never take art lessons.
c. Creativity doesn't have to be taught.
d. There are a lot of bad paintings in art galleries.

Speaker 2
a. How creative you are depends on how old you are.
b. Women are more creative in some areas than men.
c. People of all sexes and ages can be creative.
d. Creativity is not an important trait for either sex to possess.

Video Activities: A Life of Painting

Before You Watch.   Discuss these questions in small groups.

1. At what age do people usually retire?

2. Do you know any elderly people who are still working? If so, how do they feel about their work?

Watch.   Answer the following questions.

1. What was Harry Sternberg's occupation? _____

2. What is his occupation now? _____

3. Why did he move from New York City to Escondido, California?
    a. for health reasons   b. for financial reasons
    c. to be near his children   d. to be near his wife's family

4. The narrator uses a nickname for New York City. What is it? _____

5. How did Harry feel when he first moved to Escondido?
       "It was a _____!"

6. What did Harry discover when he drew pictures of people on the New York City subway? Most people hated _____.

7. How do we know that Harry loves his work?
    a. He sleeps in his studio.
    b. He sometimes forgets to eat.
    c. When he goes away, he can't wait to get back.
    d. He paints every day.
    e. He gets excited before he starts every new painting.

Watch Again.   Compare answers in small groups.

1. What are the names of the first two paintings? _____ and _____

2. Complete the name of the exhibition in the beginning of the video.
       "No _____ Without _____"

3. Listen for the numbers.
    1. the number of years Harry Sternberg has been painting   _____
    2. the number of years he lived in New York City   _____
    3. the year he moved to Escondido   _____
    4. the number of self-portraits he has painted   _____
    5. his age   _____

4. Complete the quotation.
       "I'm as _____ now when I _____ as I was _____."

After You Watch.   Discuss these questions with your class.

1. Do you think Harry Sternberg is lucky? Why or why not?

2. Would you like to work for as long as Harry Sternberg has? Why or why not?

3. Why do you think Harry Sternberg enjoys his work so much?

Chapter 9

Human Behavior

Did You Know?

■ Americans have associations for just about every interest you can imagine. Athletes United for Peace has 300 members, the International Laughter Society has 800, and there are 700,000 people in the Young American Bowling Alliance.

■ An association called the Giraffe Project has 2,500 members who "stick their necks out" to help other people in ways that involve physical, financial, or social risk.

■ Between 86% and 90% of Americans belong to an organized group or club. Seven out of ten Americans belong to at least one organization that is devoted to helping others or improving the community. These people give their time without pay to improve the lives of others.

PART 1

Getting Started

Sharing Your Experience

1   **How Sociable Are You?**   Whenever you are with other people, even one person, you are in a group.

1. Think about where you were, what you did, and who you were with one day last weekend and complete the chart.

Time	Were you alone?	Number of people you were with	Activity
8:00 A.M.			
10:00 A.M.			
12 NOON			
2:00 P.M.			
4:00 P.M.			
6:00 P.M.			
8:00 P.M.			
10:00 P.M.			
12 MIDNIGHT			

2. In small groups, answer these questions.

- How many hours were you alone?
- How many hours were you with others?
- What activity took up most of your time?

3. Discuss the following questions with the whole class.

1. What types of groups did you participate in?
2. Was this a typical day for each of you? Why or why not?
3. Are people in the class similar or different in the amount of time they spend alone and in groups?
4. Would you prefer to spend more time, less time, or the same amount of time in groups? Why?

Vocabulary Preview

2 **Vocabulary in Context.** The underlined words in the following sentences are used in the same manner as in the lecture. Below each word are three definitions. Choose the definition that best fits the word as it is used in the sentence.

Example: Many international students already have a particular <u>field of interest</u>.

a. ___ a piece of land with no trees
b. _×_ a division of academic study
c. ___ a place where oil is found

1. Joe feels his position as president of a political group on campus is an important part of his <u>identity</u>.
   a. ___ individuality, the condition of being oneself
   b. ___ intellect, intelligence
   c. ___ innocence, lack of experience

2. A number of <u>random</u> events contributed to Joe's joining the group.
   a. ___ chance
   b. ___ classical
   c. ___ cheap

3. Joe can <u>pretty much</u> do what he wants because he shares an apartment off campus and has plenty of money.
   a. ___ never
   b. ___ hardly ever
   c. ___ almost always

4. In some cultures, <u>eye contact</u> is important when speaking to someone.
   a. ___ looking directly into someone's eyes
   b. ___ agreeing with someone
   c. ___ knowing someone's eye color

5. Before Joe can go fishing with his friends, he needs to <u>wind</u> his new line around the reel.
   a. ___ to blow
   b. ___ to plant
   c. ___ to wrap

6. Joe took five minutes at the end of a group meeting to <u>recap</u> his ideas.
   a. ___ to change
   b. ___ to bottle
   c. ___ to summarize

PART 2   # Recognizing Digressions

Making a Digression

Most lecturers *digress* from time to time. That is, they go off the topic. They do this for a number of reasons:

- A lecturer might have an interesting or amusing idea that does not relate directly to the subject.
- A lecturer may want to connect a new idea to something the students already know.
- A lecturer wants to help students become more involved in a particular topic. In this case, the lecturer might suggest activities or readings students can do on their own.
- A lecturer sees the students getting tired and wants to give them a chance to relax for a few minutes.

Note:

■ Digressions are usually used for enrichment.

■ Information in digressions is not usually included on exams.

When lecturers digress too much, it can be difficult to follow the lecture. But most lecturers are careful to point out to students when they are beginning a digression. Sometimes a lecturer begins a digression by announcing it with an apology or request for permission. In such cases, the speaker may use one of the following expressions.

Expressions for Announcing Digressions

(Just) As an aside . . .	By the way . . .
If I may digress . . .	If I may stray from the subject . . .
If I may wander . . .	If you'll let me digress for a moment . . .
Let me digress . . .	Let me just mention that . . .
Let me mention in passing that . . .	Oh, I forgot to mention . . .
Oh, that makes me think of . . .	Oh, that reminds me . . .
Oh, yes . . .	To change the subject . . .
To get off the topic for a moment . . .	To go off on a tangent for a moment . . .
To wander for just a moment . . .	

Returning to the Main Topic

When completing a digression, lecturers usually use certain expressions to indicate to students that they are returning to the main topic.

Expressions That Announce a Return to the Main Topic

Anyway . . .	Anyway, as I was saying . . .
As I started to say . . .	Back to our main topic . . .
(But) Enough of . . .	To come back to what I was saying . . .
To continue with our main point . . .	To get back to the topic at hand . . .
To go on with what I was saying . . .	To return to what I was saying . . .
Well, back to business . . .	Well, back to work . . .
Well, to continue (with the main topic) . . .	

Before You Listen

1 **Discussing Digressions.**   Since you don't usually lecture to your friends, acquaintances, or relatives, informal conversations are often one digression after another. In small groups, discuss the following questions about digressions.

1. When would a digression be impolite? Are there any circumstances in which it would be impolite not to digress?

2. What are some specific reasons people might use digressions?

3. When do you think digressions are most useful?

2   **Making an Educated Guess about Digressions.**   With a partner, read the following statements from the lecture. Make an educated guess about which statements relate to the main points in the lecture and which statements are digressions. Then put a mark in the column for Main Point or Digression.

Statement	Main point	Digression	Phrase used to introduce the digression	Reason for the digression
1. "This afternoon I'm going to talk about a topic that affects every person in this room—group dynamics."	x			
2. "First we'll look at patterns of communication in groups and then we'll look at how groups affect individual performance."				
3. "You all went to the discussion session yesterday, didn't you?"				
4. "It doesn't seem to matter how large the group is—only a few people talk at once."				
5. "I must tell you that all the research I know about has been done in the United States and Canada."				
6. "The research shows that in groups of eight or more, people talk to the people sitting across the table from them."				
7. "If you're planning to be a matchmaker and start a romance between two of your friends, don't seat them next to each other at your next dinner party."				
8. "The theory behind this type of research—research that demonstrates that people do better work in groups—is called social facilitation theory."				
9. "In this way, we're like a number of other creatures."				
10. "As I mentioned earlier, there is also research that demonstrates the opposite— that individuals perform worse, not better, on tasks when other people are there."				
11. "If you don't already know how to do something, you will probably make some mistakes. And if you have an audience, you will continue to make mistakes."				
12. "If you can manage it, you should take tests on a stage in front of a large audience."				
How many items did you guess were digressions?				

Listen

3 **Listening for Digressions.**   Listen to the lecture. As you listen, check your guesses about the statements in Activity 2 by noting the phrases the lecturer uses to introduce digressions. Write them in the chart beside the digressions they introduce. Then note the reasons for the digressions. Use the following abbreviations to save time:

AI = to keep the audience interested
C   = to connect abstract ideas to real experiences
PAI = to provide additional information
R   = to relax the audience

4 **Listening for Returns to the Main Topic.**   Read the expressions in the explanation box that indicate a return to the main topic. Listen to the lecture again. As you listen, note which expressions the lecturer uses to return to the main topic from the digressions.

After You Listen

5 **Comparing Reasons for Digressions.**   Compare your findings from Activity 3 with your classmates.

1. How many digressions did each person hear?
2. Which expressions were used to introduce the digressions?
3. What was the most frequent reason for a digression?
4. What was the least frequent reason?

Talk It Over

6 **Reporting on Digressions.**

1. Sit in on a class that interests you or attend a public lecture or meeting (for example, a meeting of the Sierra Club). The newspaper probably lists the time and place of events that are open to the public. If you can't attend a lecture or meeting, listen to one on television or the radio.

2. Listen for the digressions in the lecture. When you hear a digression, make a note of the phrase used to introduce it and the reason for the digression. Use the same abbreviations that you used in Activity 3 to save time (AI, C, PAI, and R). Be careful not to confuse digressions with examples!

3. Report your findings to your class and compare notes.
    ■ How many digressions did each person hear?
    ■ What is the average number of digressions per lecture class members heard?
    ■ What was the most frequent reason for a digression?
    ■ What was the least frequent reason?

7   **Discussing Group Activities.**

1.   Work in small groups. Discuss three of the following activities that we do in groups. Add other activities to the list if you wish.

dating	going to see a band
going to the movies	investing money as a group
playing a team sport	going dancing at a nightclub
studying in a group	working on a team project
eating out	sharing a room or apartment

Write down the topics your group has chosen.

1. _____

2. _____

3. _____

2.   Discuss the topics one at a time. During the discussions, members of the group should try to get off the topic by digressing. Be sure to use expressions to introduce your digressions.

3.   If you are successful and get the group to listen to your digression, practice using appropriate expressions to return to the main point.

PART 3

Using Tag Questions to Ask for Information, Confirm, or Challenge

Tag questions are questions added or "tagged on" at the end of a statement. They are very short, usually consisting of only a subject and an auxiliary verb.

Affirmative and Negative Tag Questions

1.   If the statement is negative, the tag question is always affirmative.

         negative   affirmative

    Example: He's not coming to soccer practice today, is he?

2.   If the statement is affirmative, generally the tag question is negative.

         affirmative   negative

    Example: He's coming to soccer practice today, isn't he?

3.   But sometimes a challenging affirmative statement is followed by an affirmative tag question.

         affirmative   affirmative

    Example: He's coming to soccer practice today, is he?

Intonation plays a big part in conveying the intention of a tag question. The first two examples of tag questions might be genuine questions with rising intonation. These same tag questions could easily be changed to rhetorical questions by using falling intonation. Try it.

The third example is a challenging question (an affirmative statement with an affirmative tag question) with a sudden rising intonation.

Tag questions are used for three purposes.

Purposes of Tag Questions

1. Genuine questions (to ask for information)
Here the speaker sincerely wants to know the answer. The genuine tag question has rising intonation.

Example: You're coming to soccer practice today, aren't you?

2. Rhetorical questions (to confirm)
Here the speaker knows the answer already and just wants confirmation or agreement from the listener. The rhetorical question has falling intonation.

Example: You really know how to pass the ball, don't you?

3. Challenging questions (to challenge)
The speaker uses an affirmative statement followed by an affirmative tag to signal a challenge meaning: "You're (he's, she's, they're) not going to get away with that." The challenging tag question has rising intonation, but it rises more suddenly than the genuine question does.

Example: So they think they're going to win the match, do they?

Other Words and Phrases That Function as Tag Questions

Phrases	Examples
Okay?	You'll be the goalie today, okay?
Right?	The score is 2-2, right?
Huh?	So you thought we'd lose, huh?
Don't you think?	He plays a fine game of tennis, don't you think?
Don't you agree?	Derek Jeter is a great athlete, don't you agree?

1   **Listening for Intonation Patterns.**   Listen to the following conversations that include tag questions. Answer the questions after each conversation.

Conversation 1

Steven is telling Tom about the first soccer practice of the season, which is only two days away.

What intonation pattern does Steven use—genuine question, rhetorical question, or challenging question? _____

Conversation 2

All week, Steven and Tom have been looking forward to playing soccer on Saturday. Steven is telling a third friend, George, about the practice.

What intonation pattern does Steven use this time—genuine question, rhetorical question, or challenging question? _____

Conversation 3

Soccer practice has been arranged for 6:30 A.M. because another team has reserved the field for 8:30. Tom and Steven are talking about Karl, who told Tom that he wouldn't be coming until 8:00.

What intonation pattern does Steven use here- genuine question, rhetorical question, or challenging question? _____

Conversation 4

Charlie's boss expects a report on Friday but realizes that it would be useful at a meeting on Wednesday.

What intonation pattern does the boss use—genuine question, rhetorical question, or challenging question? _____

Conversation 5

Josie comes home and sees Peter, one of her housemates, sitting in the living room with his feet up. Since it's already 6:00, she concludes that it's not his turn to cook.

What single-word tag questions are used in this conversation? _____

2 **Listening for the Three Types of Tag Questions.**

1. Listen to the lecture again. This time, notice the tag questions. As you listen, complete the following chart.

2. When you are finished, compare your chart with those of your classmates. If there are differences, listen to the lecture again and see if you can agree this time.

	Genuine	Rhetorical	Challenging
Affirmative		Part of some group, right?	
Negative			
Other			

3 **Using Tag Questions to Confirm Information.** In groups of five to ten, get confirmation from one person at a time about his or her leisure activities. Only use statements followed by tag questions. If you are not sure what this person does during his or her leisure time, make a guess followed by a genuine tag question (with rising intonation). If you definitely know one of this person's leisure activities, make a statement followed by a rhetorical tag question.

When this person has answered all the tag questions from the group, use tag questions to get confirmation from another member of the group. Here are a few examples:

You like to play handball, don't you?	or	You don't like to play handball, do you?
You're a terrific dancer, aren't you?	or	You don't like to dance, do you?
Your collection of jazz is huge, isn't it?	or	You don't collect jazz, do you?

Talk It Over

4 **Using Tag Questions in Role-Plays.**

1. In groups of two to four, role-play a few of the following situations or create some of your own. Use as many tag questions—and *types* of tag questions—as you can. Then present your role-plays to the class.

2. Keep score of the number of genuine, rhetorical, and challenging tag questions each group uses. You might give bonus points for using challenging tags in the role-plays because these can be quite tricky to use appropriately.

3. Total the scores for each group.

    Which group used the most tag questions? _____

    Which group used the most types of tag questions? _____

    Which group used the most challenging tag questions? _____

Situations

1. During a break between sets at a show with friends, half the group thinks the band is awful and wants to leave; the other half thinks it's great and wants to stay.

2. At a restaurant, friends are deciding whether to split the bill equally, have each person pay exactly her or his share, or let one person have a turn paying the whole thing.

3. You and some friends are on a mountain camping trip. Although you had planned to stay for five days, it's starting to snow on the second day.

4. At the office, the boss has suggested a ten-hour day with a four-day work week. The employees may make the final decision, but some of them like to have long weekends, and others prefer to spread out their leisure time over the entire week.

5. At home, you've just received a phone call saying that you've won an all-expenses-paid vacation to Hawaii. You may bring one friend. Your two best friends were sitting with you when you received the call.

6. A teenager who was supposed to be home by midnight arrives home at 3:00 A.M. The teenager doesn't want to be grounded (a punishment in which the young person can't leave the house except to go to school), so he or she tries to tiptoe quietly into the house. One of the parents, however, has come downstairs for a snack, and the teenager and the parent bump right into each other.

7. On your vacation you take an airplane. You try to start a conversation with the attractive person next to you, but a naughty child is making a lot of noise and keeps interrupting you. The parent doesn't seem to be anywhere around.

PART 4   # Focus on Testing

Listen to the two conversations. After each conversation, you will hear a question. Circle the letter of the best answer to each question.

Conversation 1
a. On a tennis court.
b. On a racquetball court.
c. In a sporting goods store.
d. On a golf course.

Conversation 2
a. Tom doesn't have many people on his side.
b. Tom can't possibly win the election.
c. Tom will win if the special interest groups vote for him.
d. Tom is certain to win the election.

Video Activities: People Skills

Before You Watch.   Discuss these questions in small groups.

1.   How do people greet each other in different cultures?

2.   Which of these do you think are "people skills"?

    a.   being a good listener   b.   being athletic
    c.   being a good actor   d.   being smart

Watch.   Answer the following questions.

1.   The reporter says that this is National _____ Month
    a.   People to People   b.   Friendly People   c.   People Skills

2.   Match the types of handshakes with the descriptions.
    1.   wimpy   a.   too strong
    2.   bonecrusher   b.   correct strength
    3.   perfect   c.   too weak

3.   The telephone game shows that most people _____.
    a.   don't have good memories   b.   don't speak clearly
    c.   aren't good listeners   d.   aren't competitive

4.   Here is the message used in the telephone game. How did it change?
    The Jenkins project will be put on hold for three weeks until Connie's digital
    pager returns from the shop in Ohio.

    _____

    _____

Watch Again.   Compare answers in small groups.

1.   The man in the video thinks that his handshake is _____.
    a. wimpy   b.   perfect   c.   a bonecrusher

2.   The man he shakes hands with thinks that it is _____.
    a. wimpy   b.   perfect   c.   a bonecrusher

3.   What are the names of the people the woman has to remember?
    _____   _____   _____

4.   The woman says, "…you put me on the spot!"
    She means that the reporter _____.
    a.   tricked her
    b.   made her stand in the wrong place
    c.   asked her a difficult question

After You Watch.

1.   Shake hands with a few students in your classroom. What kinds of handshakes
do they have? Do you think a firm (strong) handshake is important? Why or
why not?

2.   Play telephone with your classmates. Are you good listeners or not?

32% of health impacts are within 30 miles of the plant

Air Pollution Promotes the Spread of CANCER Salem has the Highest Cancer Incidence Rate in the Region.

Chapter 10

Crime and Punishment

Did You Know?

- On December 1, 1955, Rosa Parks, a 42-year-old African American seamstress, chose to break the law in Montgomery, Alabama. She was ordered by a city bus driver to give up her seat to a white man, as was then required by the city's racial segregation laws. She refused and was arrested. Four days later, the African American community, led by Dr. Martin Luther King Jr., began a boycott of the city bus company that lasted 382 days. Finally, the U.S. Supreme Court ruled that racial segregation on city buses was unconstitutional. Because of her role in starting the successful boycott, Rosa Parks became known as the "mother of the civil rights movement."

- The longest known prison sentence ever given out by a judge was 141,078 years. A Thai woman and seven associates each received this sentence in Bangkok Criminal Court in 1989. Their crime: cheating the public through a fake deposit-taking business.

- Recent studies of the death penalty in the United States show that, contrary to expectations, states that use the death penalty as punishment for the crime of murder have higher murder rates than do states that do not use it.

PART 1

Getting Started

Sharing Your Experience

Work in small groups to complete the following activities.

1 Have you ever considered doing something you knew was wrong in order to get something you wanted? For example, pretending to be sick in order to get a day off or taking something from a store without paying for it. What did you consider doing? What was the result? Share one or two stories with the whole class.

2 In the first column, list several things that are against the law. Next to each illegal act, list the punishment that is usually given for breaking this law. Then talk about these crimes and punishments. Which ones do you think are fair? Which ones are not? Why not? Share the key points of your group discussions with the whole class.

The Crime	The Punishment
_____	_____
_____	_____
_____	_____
_____	_____

Vocabulary Preview

3 **Definitions.**   You will hear these words in the lecture. Before you listen, work with a partner and write the letter of the correct definition beside each word.

____ 1. free will	a. rebirth in new bodies or forms of life
____ 2. karma	b. controlled by a plan
____ 3. life-and-death	c. infraction; illegality
____ 4. predetermination	d. regret for doing something wrong
____ 5. programmed	e. freedom of humans to make choices that are not determined by outside influences
____ 6. reincarnation	f. the belief that all events in a person's life have already been decided
____ 7. remorse	g. the principle that determines what will happen to us in the future, including our form in our next life; it is based on the belief that our choices add up to either a good life or a bad one
____ 8. violation	h. very important, as if involving life and death

PART 2 # Paraphrasing

Paraphrasing is restating an idea using different words. In class, you may be asked to restate in your own words something the instructor said or that you read in your textbook. Paraphrasing is a useful study skill because it helps you remember ideas and concepts that you learn.

Before You Listen

1 **Considering the Topic.**   Predetermination and free will are key concepts discussed by the lecturer. Read the following list of activities with a partner. Think about each one. Which ones do you freely choose? Which ones do you not get to choose? Decide whether each one is an example of predetermination or free will and put a check in the corresponding column. Add at least one item to the list for each category. Share the highlights of your discussion with the whole class.

Activity	Predetermination	Free will
going to the movies		
going to school		
how you travel to school		
choosing a marriage partner		
whether to work or not		
your nationality		
your religion		

2   Paraphrasing.   Rewrite the following sentences in your own words. Do not use your dictionary. Try to get the meaning from the sentence and make an educated guess. Then compare answers with your classmates. Use a dictionary only if there are important differences among the answers.

Example: "The unexamined life is not worth living."   —*Socrates*

If you don't look closely at your own behavior, your life will be meaningless.

1. Maybe we are programmed to do the things we do.

_____

_____

_____

2. If you feel that you are not in control, then you might also feel that you do not have to take responsibility for your choices.

_____

_____

_____

3. Our relationship to the past and to the future seems to be connected with our present choices.

_____

_____

_____

4. The practical implications of choice increase and intensify when life-or-death decisions have to be made.

_____

_____

_____

5. We only punish people who choose consciously, willfully, and freely to commit crimes.

_____

_____

_____

Listen

3 **Listening to Paraphrase Parts of a Lecture.**   Listen to the lecture and paraphrase, or restate, the following sections. Your teacher will stop the tape after each section.

1. Listen and paraphrase what the professor says about predetermination and free will.

    _____

    _____

    _____

    _____

    _____

2. Listen and paraphrase the views about decisions involving criminal offenses. The example given is of a judge sentencing a person to prison for violation of rules in a community.

    _____

    _____

    _____

    _____

    _____

3. Listen and paraphrase the views presented on John Hinckley Jr., who was not sent to prison for his actions.

    _____

    _____

    _____

    _____

    _____

4. Listen and paraphrase the views presented on the everyday choices we all have to make, and the professor's final comments.

    _____

    _____

    _____

    _____

    _____

After You Listen

4 **Comparing Notes.**   Listen to the whole lecture once again to check your work. Then share your work in small groups by reading it aloud. How did your paraphrasing differ from that of your classmates?

Talk It Over

5 **Paraphrasing Problems for Group Discussion.**   You may have heard this quotation: "You can never say *yes* to something without saying *no* to something else." Real-life situations often force us to make unpleasant choices and to give up things we want.

1. Work in groups of three or four. Only one person in the group looks at the text-book. This person reads one of the following problem situations silently and then paraphrases it for the group. Do not mention the possible solutions given in the book at this time.
2. All group members then clarify what the problem is and discuss what they would do about it and why.
3. The first person then reads aloud the possible solutions given in the book. The group discusses the pros and cons of any of these solutions that group members did not mention earlier.
4. Another person takes the textbook, chooses another problem from the list, and repeats steps 1 through 3 with the group.

Problem Situations

1. You're having dinner with an American family. Everything goes well until they bring in the main course: steak. You don't eat meat.

    What would you do?

    a. tell them you're not hungry
    b. explain why you don't eat meat
    c. eat the meal
    d. tell them why they should not eat meat

2. You're standing in the checkout line in a market when you notice a person in the line next to you take two small candy bars out of the shopping basket and put them into his or her coat pocket.

    What would you do?

    a. tell the person to pay for them
    b. tell the checkout clerk what just happened
    c. clear your throat and stare at the person
    d. ignore the situation

3. The subject matter for a course you are taking is extremely difficult. Your friend, who took the same course last semester, says that the final is absolutely impossible but that you might pass it with a little "help"—that is, if your friend tells you what will be on the test.

   What would you do?

   a. let your friend give you the answers to the test
   b. let your friend give you some hints but not tell you all the answers
   c. not accept any help from your friend
   d. report your friend's offer to the instructor

4. You work in a large computer corporation and are in charge of hiring new employees. You must choose a new office manager from two candidates. One is a long-time friend who is new to the company; the other is a first-rate worker who has been with the company for eight years.

   What would you do?

   a. offer your friend the position
   b. offer the long-term, first-rate employee the job
   c. look for a third candidate from outside the company
   d. resign from the company and look for a new job

5. The speed limit on the highway is 55 mph. All the cars around you are going at least 65 or 70 mph, so you decide to move along with the rest of the traffic at about 68 mph. All of a sudden, you hear a siren and see the swirling blue lights of a police car behind you. You pull over to the side of the road with the police car right behind you. The police officer asks you why you were going so fast.

   What would you say?

   a. I was staying with the flow of traffic.
   b. Why did you stop me? That guy in the Porsche was going even faster.
   c. I'm sorry. I'm a foreigner and I don't understand the laws here.
   d. I'm sorry, but I'm on the way to the hospital to see a very sick relative.

PART 3

Expressing Wishes, Hopes, and Desires

The lecturer in this chapter wants his students to seriously consider the choices they make and the underlying reasons for these choices. He uses a variety of expressions to indicate wishes, hopes, and desires during the lecture.

Ways to Express Wishes, Hopes, and Desires	
I wish…	I want…
If only…	I could use…
I hope…	I need…

1 **Listening for Wishes, Hopes, and Desires.**   Listen for expressions of wishes, hopes, and desires in the following conversation. Write down all the expressions you hear. Compare notes with your classmates.

_____

_____

_____

_____

2 **Listening to Paraphrase Wishes, Hopes, and Desires.**   Read the following six items before you listen to the lecture once more. Then listen for the expressions in the lecture and complete the sentences, using your own words to paraphrase the lecturer. Stop the tape if necessary.

1. The lecturer *hopes* that by the end of class, the students understand

_____

_____

_____

2. He *wants* to hear the students' ideas about

_____

_____

_____

_____

3. The lecturer asks the students how many of them have looked at their past actions and said, "I *wish*

_____

_____

_____

_____

Or "*If only*

_____

_____

_____

_____

_____

4. The lecturer does not want to focus on Hinkley's punishment; he *wants*

_____

_____

5. In summary, he *hopes* the lecture

_____

_____

_____

_____

3 **Expressing Hopes and Wishes.** Complete the following sentences. Then share your answers with a partner or in small groups.

1. I wish I were _____

2. All I really need is _____

3. If only I had _____

4. I want to make better choices in my life. I hope to do this by _____.

Talk It Over

4 **Role-Play.**

1. Situations often come up in which you must express your hopes and desires or ask for what you want. Role-play the following three situations with a partner. Use a variety of expressions to express your wishes. Be careful not to sound impolite. Present one situation to the whole class.

Situations

■ It is the first day of a course on criminal law. You've been hoping to take the class for a long time, but you haven't had the time or the money to do it until now. The instructor begins the class by asking you to tell her or him what you hope to get from the course.

■ Lucky you! You have been selected for a job interview for a position as a translator for the World Court. The interviewer asks what you hope to gain from your experience as a translator. Then ask the interviewer what qualities she or he hopes to find in an employee.

■ You are planning a surprise birthday party for a friend. Your guests will arrive at 6:00 P.M. It's 5:30 P.M. now, and you realize that you have no ice. You run to your nearby market to get the ice. Unfortunately, there are ten people in the check-out line ahead of you. It looks like you're going to be late for the party at your own house. Then you notice that the ice is near the exit and everyone seems to be looking the other way. What might your hopes and wishes be in this situation? Express your thoughts to the person in line next to you.

2. In small groups, role-play the following situation, with each person choosing a different character and expressing the wishes and hopes of the various people involved. You can use phrases like these:

I wish...	He needs...
I hope...	If only he...
If only he had/hadn't...	He could use...

Charles Burke is on trial for murder. He was a wonderful child and did well in school. At nineteen he was drafted into the army and was sent to fight in Vietnam. Two years later he returned home and tried to pick up where he'd left off, but things were never the same again for Charles.

He became angry easily and he was soon thrown out of school for fighting with a professor. He was fired from several jobs. He wanted to meet a nice girl and get married, but he couldn't seem to get close to anyone. Finally, one day Charles shot someone for "no reason."

Charles's lawyer hopes that Charles will not be held responsible for his crime. He hopes that the judge and jury will understand that at the moment of the shooting, Charles did not know right from wrong, that he was temporarily insane and did not consciously choose to commit murder.

The following people are being interviewed by CNN:

Charles Burke	Charles's best friend from school
Charles's lawyer	Charles's kind grade school teacher
the prosecuting attorney	the judge
Charles's mother or father	a dismissed jury member, who was released in
the wife of the murdered man	the middle of the trial and is now allowed to give interviews to the news media

---

PART 4	# Focus on Testing

Listen to the two conversations. After each conversation, you will hear a question. Circle the letter of the best answer to each question.

Conversation 1

a.   If you want to commit a crime, don't tell me about it.
b.   If you want to steal a car, don't go to jail.
c.   If you aren't ready to take the consequences, don't do it.
d.   If you commit a crime, you can't get caught.

Conversation 2

a.   You should believe what older people tell you.
b.   There might be a bad side to getting what you wish for.
c.   You will probably become famous someday.
d.   You will be very disappointed if you don't get what you wish for.

Video Activities: Victim Support Groups

Before You Watch.   Discuss these questions in small groups.

1.   What do you think a support group is? Who is in it? What is its purpose?

2.   What murderer cases have you heard about? What was the punishment? Do you think it was fair?

3.   In most countries, convicted criminals have the right to appeal their conviction. What do you think *appeal* means?

Watch.   Answer the following questions.

1. The video is about a support group for _____.
    a. families of murderers
    b. murder victims
    c. families of murder victims
    d. murderers

2. Who are the "monsters" referred to the video? _____

3. According to Susan Field, how is murder different from a natural death for the victim's family?
    a. The grief period is longer.
    b. They feel angrier.
    c. There is a lot of publicity.
    d. They have had no time to prepare for it.
    e. They have to deal with the judicial system.

4. According to Jim Roche, what should the United States Supreme Court do to help the families of murder victims?
    a. Put more murderers in prison.
    b. Change the appeal process.
    c. Stop all appeals.
    d. Get rid of the death penalty.

5. According to Kate Elke, execution is state law and it should be _____.
    a. changed
    b. abolished
    c. enforced

Watch Again.   Compare answers in small groups.

1. Write these names in the correct row.

Ron Russe	Susan Fisher	Linda Ricio	Virginia Allen
Pamela Allen	Sammy Smith	Kate Elke	Jim Roche

Murder Victim   _____

Murderer   _____

Relative of Murder Victim   _____

Government Official   _____

After You Watch.   Discuss these questions with your class.

1. Do you agree with capital punishment (the death penalty)? Why or why not? If you agree, what crimes deserve capital punishment?

2. Would you ever join a support group such as the one talked about in the video? Why or why not?

Chapter 11

The Physical World

Did You Know?

- The first people to reach the South Pole were five Norwegian men led by Captain Roald Amundsen on December 4, 1911. They traveled 55 days by dog sled to get there.
- The first people to reach the North Pole were three Russian explorers who arrived and departed by air on April 23, 1968.
- The north and south polar regions balance the flow of air and water for the entire planet. Without this balance, we would face catastrophic floods and droughts (dry periods) that would change the face of the earth. In fact, if enough ice at the poles melts, an inland desert such as the one surrounding Las Vegas, Nevada, might eventually become beachfront property.

PART 1

Getting Started

Sharing Your Experience

1 Work in groups of three. Imagine that you are a zoologist about to begin a study of penguins with two other scientists. To prepare for your field study, which will include trips to Antarctica, discuss the following details with your colleagues. Write the details of your discussion in the following chart. When you are finished, compare your chart with those of other groups.

Facts about penguins we want to learn	Who we will take with us and why	Supplies needed	Where we will go first, second, etc.	How we will travel	How much time needed in each place	Dangers we will face	Times we will observe penguins

Vocabulary Preview

2 **Vocabulary in Context.**   Check your knowledge of the underlined vocabulary words in the following sentences that will appear in the lecture. If the underlined word is used correctly, mark the sentence with a C. If it is used incorrectly, mark the sentence with an I. With a partner, compare answers and confirm them with a dictionary.

1. __C__ Because I like <u>desolate</u> places, I'm thinking of becoming a hermit and moving to Antarctica.

2. __I__ Inland in Antarctica you can find beautiful <u>beachfront</u> property.

3. _____ <u>Catastrophic</u> floods could change the biological patterns of the world.

4. _____ <u>Migratory</u> birds cannot fly.

5. _____ The term <u>ecosystem</u> refers to a network of relationships among organisms that are interdependent.

6. _____ A temperature of 32 degrees <u>Fahrenheit</u> is 0 degrees <u>Celsius</u>.

7. _____ Some birds eat a lot and build up fat reserves in preparation for a long <u>fast</u>.

8. _____ Once penguin chicks begin to hatch, the colony begins to <u>teem</u> with life.

9. _____ The penguin's <u>disposition</u> is black and white.

10. _____ A <u>ferocious</u> attack by a sea leopard might kill a penguin.

11. _____ The <u>brooding</u> instinct is very strong in penguins.

12. _____ On land penguins seem very <u>awkward</u>, but in the water they move very gracefully.

PART 2   Outlining

Information can be organized and shortened for study by putting it in outline form. Outlining highlights the main ideas and supporting information found in a reading passage or an oral presentation (such as a class lecture). Following is a typical outline format.

I. _____

    A. _____

    B. _____

II. _____

    A. _____

    B. _____

III. _____

    A. _____

        1. _____

        2. _____

    B. _____

This format can vary, depending on how the material is organized. However, the main points are always represented by Roman numerals (I, II, III, etc.), and less important points are represented by capital letters (A, B, C, etc.). Minor points are represented by Arabic numerals (1, 2, 3, etc.).

Before You Listen

1 **Predicting Main Ideas and Supporting Information.**   Before you listen to the lecture about penguins, study the following partial outline of information about their mating and brooding habits. With a partner, try to guess what kind of information is missing from the outline.

I. Mating habits of penguins

    A. Need for order leads penguins to build nests in rows

    B. Order is often interrupted by small wars between males

        1. _____

        2. _____

    C. _____

    D. Losers move to edge of nesting ground

Listen

2 **Listening for Main Ideas and Supporting Information.**   Listen to the lecture on penguins. Pay special attention to the information about mating habits. Then, with a partner, listen to the first part of the lecture again and fill in the information missing from the previous outline.

3 **Constructing an Outline as You Listen.**   Listen to the lecture again. This time pay special attention to the information about brooding. With a partner, complete an outline of this information on the lines provided here. Be sure to include in your outline (1) the reasons for the high casualty rate of eggs, (2) what happens when chicks hatch, and (3) cooperative parenting activities.

II. Penguin brooding

_____

_____

_____

_____

_____

_____

_____

_____

4 After You Listen

Comparing Outlines.   Compare your outlines of the information on penguin mating and brooding habits with those of your classmates.

Talk It Over

5 **Speaking from an Outline.**   In this activity you will have an opportunity to present your views on a topic in a more formal way. Organize your thoughts about the topic by first discussing various aspects of it and then outlining your main points.

In the ecosystem discussed in the lecture, penguins are lucky in one way: Their major enemy, the sea leopard, does not use technology to hunt them. This is not true for some of the creatures that people hunt. For example, the use of technology to kill whales has caused worldwide controversy. Discuss the following questions:

1.   Why are whales hunted? What parts of the whale are used?
2.   What methods are used to hunt whales?
3.   What is Greenpeace? What does it do?

Now decide what *your* position is on the following issues.

1.   Are the methods used to hunt whales acceptable or not?
2.   Should governments control the way in which whales are hunted? The way in which all creatures are hunted?
3.   Should whales and other endangered species be protected?
4.   Do you support the philosophy of Greenpeace? Its methods?

Make a brief outline of your views and why you feel this way. Your position on each issue is a main idea and should be listed after a Roman numeral. Under the Roman numerals, other less important information that supports each main idea can be listed after capital letters and Arabic numerals. Using only your outline as notes, present your views to your classmates and explain your reasons for your point of view.

Stating Reasons

The lecture in this chapter contains words used to emphasize the reasons why penguins exhibit certain behaviors—why they do what they do. These words are also commonly used in everyday conversations to emphasize the reasons for things.

Words Used to State Reasons

because (of)	on account of this	since
for this reason	seeing as how (very informal)	owing to
in view of that fact	the reason is (that)	

1   Listening for Ways to State Reasons.   Listen to the following conversation, which contains several different ways of stating reasons. List all the expressions used to state reasons on the following lines. Compare your list with your classmates' lists.

_____

_____

_____

_____

2   Listening for Expressions to State Reasons.   Listen to the lecture again. Notice how certain expressions make it easy for you to pick out the reasons being given. Complete each of the following sentences with the correct reason from the lecture and with an expression from the list provided here. When you are finished, compare your answers with those of your classmates.

because
because of (the fact that)
for this reason
in view of that fact
in view of the fact that
on account of (the fact that)
owing to (the fact that)
since

1.   It is not surprising to the lecturer that everyone seems more cheerful when they hear that the lecture will be about penguins _____ no one can resist these awkward little creatures dressed in _____.

2.   _____ Antarctica is a huge, desolate _____, only the strongest forms of life survive there.

3. _____ penguins are _____, _____ and _____, they are thought of as treasures of the Antarctic.

4. The penguins arrive in Antarctica in the spring with a store of _____ to carry them through the next few months _____ they have eaten a lot of _____ in warmer waters in the previous months.

5. _____ these fat reserves, they are able to swim _____ to the _____.

6. _____ as many as 50,000 birds may gather at a time, there is definitely a need for _____.

7. _____ this need, penguins build nests in such perfect rows that the nesting area looks like _____.

8. _____ the mating battles that continue for several weeks, it is not unusual to see bloodstains and _____.

9. Some males become hooligans and steal _____, disturb _____, and play jokes on the penguin couples _____ they did not find suitable mates.

10. Although the brooding instinct is very strong and parental care is truly dedicated, as many as 75% of the eggs are lost _____ catastrophic _____, death of the _____, destruction of the nests by _____, bad behavior of the _____, or the eggs being eaten by _____.

11. It is not all fun and games _____ there is not very much the penguins can do to protect themselves from _____.

12. Even though penguins are excellent swimmers, it is difficult for them to escape these ferocious attackers _____ sea leopards have _____, an _____ and _____.

13. _____ the group of penguins is smaller when it returns to the _____ the next spring.

14. Food is shared with orphaned chicks _____ penguins are _____.

Talk It Over

3   **Stating Reasons.**   Zoos and wild animal parks provide people in urban areas with the opportunity to observe wild creatures. To practice the words you studied in the previous exercises, do one of the following activities in small groups.

1.   If you have been to a zoo or wild animal park, describe it to your classmates. Use the words for stating reasons and answer these questions:

   ■   Why do you think the zoo or park was built?
   ■   Why did you go there? Why do most people go there?
   ■   Did you think the animals were content, or did you think they would be happier in the wild? Why?
   ■   Were the animals well cared for?
   ■   Do you think it is acceptable to restrict wild animals' natural behaviors by keeping them in an artificial environment?

2.   If you have not been to a zoo or animal park, consider the questions in No. 1 based on what you have heard or read. Then decide whether you are in favor of or against zoos and wild animal parks. Tell why, using at least three of the expressions for stating reasons.

4   **What You Would Do and Why.**   If you could study any creature on earth in the wild, what would it be? Discuss why you would like to take a field trip to study this creature. Use the expressions for stating reasons. What facts about this creature would you want to learn before the trip? What specific behaviors would you want to watch for during the trip and why?

PART 4   # Focus on Testing

Listen to the two conversations. After each conversation, you will hear a question. Circle the letter of the best answer to each question.

Conversation 1
a.   a teaching job at Elmhurst College
b.   a chance to join the Antarctica expedition
c.   a chance to join another expedition
d.   to be cut from the teaching staff at the college

Conversation 2
a.   People in the Polar Regions are in danger.
b.   People should pay more attention to polar bears.
c.   The ecology of the Polar Regions is important to everyone.
d.   People who live near the Polar Regions are not ecologists.

Video Activities: Air Pollution

Before You Watch.   Answer the following questions in small groups.

1. Smog is a kind of _____ pollution.
    a. air   b. water   c. noise

2. What causes smog?
    a. cars and factories   b. bad weather   c. construction

3. What problems does smog cause?

Watch. Answer the following questions.

1. The Environmental Protection Agency's new rules will _____ air pollution.
    a. decrease   b. eliminate   c. cause

2. How does the oil industry feel about the new rules? Why?

3. The new rules will make diesel fuel _____.
    a. cleaner and cheaper
    b. less expensive but more dangerous
    c. safer but more expensive

Watch Again.

1. The EPA's new rules will decrease sulphur emissions by _____.
    a. 90%   b. 7%   c. 97%

2. The EPA is particularly worried about emissions from which two kinds of vehicles?
    a. cars
    b. trucks
    c. motorcycle
    d. buses
    e. motorhomes

3. According to an official from the oil industry the new rules will create new national standards that the industry cannot _____ for a _____ that fuel distributions systems cannot _____ at _____ American consumers cannot _____.

4. What diseases does air pollution cause?
    a. cancer   b. tuberculosis   c. malaria   d. asthma

5. When do the new rules start go into effect?

6. How long will old vehicles be on the roads?

After You Watch. Discuss these questions with your class.

1. Is air pollution a problem in your community? Are some places worse than others?

2. What is the government trying to do about air pollution? Are their rules effective? Why or why not? Are they controversial? Why or why not?

Chapter 12

Together on a Small Planet

Did You Know?

■ A researcher found that 85% of surveyed Americans believed they have a "good sense of humor." This statistic does not tell us whether these people have actually do have a good sense of humor, but it does tell us that Americans value humor.

■ North Americans almost always give a brief apology or introduction before telling a joke. These apologies are called disclaimers. One survey has shown that the average number of disclaimers made before telling a joke is 1.9 for men and 3.4 for women.

■ When a comedian, such as Robin Williams, stands up and tells jokes for 40 minutes, he or she averages about 245 jokes. That's about 6 jokes a minute.

PART 1

Getting Started

Sharing Your Experience

1   **Discussing Humor.**   Discuss the following questions in small groups. Each group should choose someone to take notes and give a short report about the discussions to the class.

1. What makes people laugh? Do people laugh mostly at real events or at made-up jokes? Is the humor mainly verbal or is it visual? Describe a humorous television show or a comedian you like.

2. Are teachers who get students to laugh more effective in helping students learn? Why or why not?

Scene from the classic American TV comedy, "I Love Lucy."

Vocabulary Preview

2   **Vocabulary in Context.**   The speaker uses the following vocabulary in the lecture. Discuss the meaning of each word with a partner. Then choose the sentence in which the underlined word is used correctly.

ain't	*nonstandard English contraction of* am not, is not, *or* are not
belly	*stomach area; abdomen*
colloquial	*characteristic of informal rather than formal English*
conscience	*feeling of moral responsibility*
folly	*foolishness*
hain't	*nonstandard English contraction of* has not *or* have not
harsh	*very unpleasant, severe, cruel*
impromptu	*made or done without planning; spontaneous*
moderation	*not too much; a reasonable amount*
moralist	*a person who comments on what is right and wrong*
prudence	*cautious judgment in practical matters*

1. folly

   _____ a. A student's <u>folly</u> will probably help the student make friends.

   _____ b. Generally, people see the <u>folly</u> right after summer when the leaves turn red and gold.

   _X_ c. A friend may sometimes help us see the <u>folly</u> of our ways.

2. moderation

   _____ a. Because Chang ate in <u>moderation</u>, he never got fat.

   _____ b. He left his <u>moderation</u> on the counter at the bank.

   _____ c. Practicing <u>moderation</u>, Sam spent all of his paycheck the day he got it.

3. moralist

   _____ a. The advice of a <u>moralist</u> can be helpful and at the same time quite annoying.

   _____ b. A <u>moralist</u> is someone who always takes a second serving of food at dinner.

   _____ c. The ecological study of the moors in England was done by a qualified <u>moralist</u>.

4. belly

   _____ a. The child ate a very green apple and got a pain in her <u>belly</u>.

   _____ b. He rang the <u>belly</u> so hard he almost fell over.

   _____ c. She wore a beautiful bell-shaped dress to the dance and was the <u>belly</u> of the ball.

5. colloquial

_____ a. His <u>colloquial</u> dress made him stand out from the rest of the group.

_____ b. His manner of speaking was very <u>colloquial</u>, but since this was an informal situation it was quite all right.

_____ c. He was known to everyone in town as a <u>colloquial</u> character.

6. conscience

_____ a. The idea was very <u>conscience</u>, not at all abstract.

_____ b. His <u>conscience</u> was aching, so his wife gave him an aspirin.

_____ c. His <u>conscience</u> told him to turn over to the lost and found department the $500 he picked up in front of the cafeteria.

7. harsh

_____ a. <u>Harshness</u> is something parents try to develop in their children.

_____ b. The <u>harsh</u> in his neck stuck out whenever he got angry.

_____ c. His <u>harshness</u> was unbelievable! He never once considered how cruel his criticism sounded to her.

8. impromptu

_____ a. He got up early and put on an <u>impromptu</u> robe.

_____ b. Most people believe making an <u>impromptu</u> speech is difficult.

_____ c. He stayed up late at night and got up early every morning, leading an <u>impromptu</u> life.

9. prudence

_____ a. She left her <u>prudence</u> in the refrigerator to chill.

_____ b. She always made <u>prudent</u> decisions about her health.

_____ c. She had not yet <u>prudent</u> her point when the teacher ended the discussion.

PART 2

Summarizing

Consider these situations:

■ You have just read an excellent book and want to tell a friend about it.

■ You have seen a thrilling movie and want to persuade your instructor to go see it.

■ You have heard a fantastic lecture and want to share your newfound knowledge with a roommate.

How can you best convey this type of information? You can tell everything you remember about the book, movie, or lecture, but it's probably better just to tell your listener about the major points. This is called *summarizing*. Throughout this book you have been developing skills to help you summarize.

For example, you have learned to:

- listen for the main idea
- listen for key terms
- outline
- paraphrase

To create a good summary—one that is both accurate and concise—you need to follow two steps:

1. Gather information by reading, taking notes, or listening carefully for the main points or highlights.
2. Organize your thoughts carefully so that your summary is as brief as possible but still accurate and complete.

Think about your audience. If you are presenting your summary to an instructor, think about clues your instructor might have given you during the lecture to indicate what he or she considers especially important. If you are summarizing a movie for a friend, you can be less thorough. For example, you might describe one scene in detail and skip several important ones. Or you might choose to not give away the surprise ending.

Terms That Signal a Repetition or Summary of Important Points

in sum	in summary
to sum up	to summarize

Part of the task of summarizing is knowing what to include and what to leave out. For example:

- There is no need to summarize jokes, interruptions, or other digressions in a lecture.
- Generally, you should not try to summarize a short quotation. If the quotation is carefully worded and states a main point, your summary could end up being longer than the original quotation.

Before You Listen

1 **Sharing Folk Wisdom and Advice.**   Share your answers to the following questions in small groups. Then share the highlights of your group discussion with the class.

1. Most cultures pass on their folk wisdom through humorous sayings that children learn as they grow up. "Don't bite the hand that feeds you" and "Look before you leap" are two common English proverbs. Do you know of similar sayings in other cultures? Are they meant to be humorous?

2. Think of advice that your mother, father, grandparents, or perhaps a wise uncle or aunt has given to you. Share this advice with your group. Is any of this advice humorous? If so, why do you think so? Can you explain what makes it funny?

Listen

2   **Summarizing Lecture Notes.** Listen to the lecture once to get the main ideas. Then listen again and take notes. Finally, write a short summary about the following people, including information about their lifestyles and humorous sayings.

1. Benjamin Franklin

_____

_____

_____

_____

_____

_____

_____

2. Abraham Lincoln

_____

_____

_____

_____

_____

_____

_____

3. Mark Twain

_____

_____

_____

_____

_____

_____

_____

After You Listen

3   **Comparing Summaries.**   Compare your summaries from Activity 2 with a partner. Repeat this activity with at least two more classmates.

Talk It Over

4   **Making Up Sayings.**   Each of the following sayings should sum up one aspect of life. In small groups, think of ways to complete each sentence. When you have finished, choose one or two of the group's favorites to share with the class.

1.   Two people can keep a secret if . . .

Example: . . . one lives on a houseboat in Antarctica and the other lives in Siberia, and neither one has a telephone or mail service.

2.   People will forgive others anything except . . .

_____

_____

3.   If you want something done well . . .

_____

_____

4.   There are three kinds of teachers . . .

_____

_____

5.   There are only three things necessary to keep your partner (husband, wife, boyfriend, or girlfriend) happy . . .

_____

_____

6.   When angry, count to four; when very angry . . .

_____

_____

7.   Sometimes I feel as out of place as . . .

_____

_____

8.   Every person with an idea also has . . .

_____

_____

5 **Role-Plays.**   Read the following quotations. In small groups, create short role-plays that illustrate the main ideas of the quotations. Don't tell the rest of the class which quotation you are acting out. Allow the class to guess which quotation best summarizes your skit.

1. Everyone is ignorant—only on different subjects.—*Will Rogers*

2. Everything is funny as long as it's happening to someone else.—*Will Rogers*

3. Do not do unto others as you . . . (want them to) do unto you. Their tastes may not be the same.—*G. B. Shaw*

4. A loving person lives in a loving world. A hostile person lives in a hostile world: Everyone you meet is your mirror.—*Ken Keyes Jr.*

5. I believe I found the missing link between animal and civilized man. It is us. —*Konrad Lorenz*

6. The worst sin towards our fellow creatures is not to hate them, but to be indifferent to them; that's the essence of inhumanity.—*G. B. Shaw*

7. I've known a lot of troubles in my time—and most of them never happened.—*Mark Twain*

8. You can look at a cup as being either half empty or half full.—*proverb*

9. A bore is a man who, when you ask him how he is, tells you.—*Burt Leston Taylor*

10. Better to be quarreling than lonesome.—*Irish proverb*

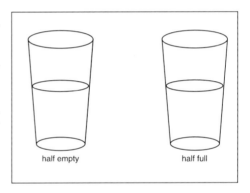

Telling a Joke

How to Introduce a Joke

Humor is valued in English-speaking countries, and it is common to hear your doctor, dentist, teacher, friends, or acquaintances tell jokes. Sharing laughter is a good way to put other people at ease and help create harmony.

People usually indicate when they are about to tell a joke. They may apologize or use a disclaimer such as "Stop me if you've heard this one before," or following "You may not think this is as funny as I do but . . ." Or they may use one of the following phrases when introducing a joke. Lecturers often do this so that the audience will relax and listen and not worry about taking notes.

Phrases Used to Introduce Jokes

Did you hear the one about . . . ?   Let me tell you the one about . . .

Have you heard . . . ?   Once there was . . .

Have you heard the one about . . . ?   Speaking about . . .

I like the one about . . .   That reminds me of the one about . . .

I love to tell the one about . . .

1 **Listening for Expressions That Introduce Jokes.** You will hear a group of students who are hanging out in the student union, telling jokes. As you listen, notice how the students introduce the four jokes they tell. Then answer the questions.

1. Catherine tells a joke that she heard her teacher tell. How does Catherine introduce the joke?

   _____

   _____

2. Jimmy tells a joke about a boy in New York City. How does Jimmy introduce his joke?

   _____

   _____

3. Joanna tells a joke about a man in a restaurant. How does Joanna introduce her joke?

   _____

   _____

4. Frank tells a joke about a little girl. How does Frank introduce the joke?

   _____

   _____

2 **Listening for Pauses That Introduce Quotations.**

1. Listen to the lecture again. Because the lecturer uses quotations from famous people and not jokes, he does not indicate when the humor is coming with comments such as "Let me tell you the one about." However, he does pause and change the rhythm or pace of his speaking.

2. Use these pauses and changes in rhythm and pace as cues to help you listen for the humor and the quotations. Write down key words in the quotations so that you can use them in your conversations later. To help you, the first five words are given. Use short forms and abbreviations where possible.

Quotations

Franklin

1. Early to bed and early to rise. . .
   makes a man healthy, wealth, and wise _____

2. Keep your eyes wide open before marriage. . . _____
   _____

3. Three may keep a secret. . . _____
   _____

4. Nothing is more fatal to health. . . _____
   _____

Crockett

5. "Make sure you're right, then. . . _____
   _____

Lincoln

6. "You can fool all of the people some of the time. . . _____
   _____

7. "The Lord prefers common-looking people. . . _____
   _____

Twain

8. "Hain't we got all the fools in town on our side. . . _____
   _____

9. "There are three kinds of lies. . . _____
   _____

10. "The reports of my death. . . _____
    _____

Talk It Over

3 **Telling Jokes.** Do you know someone who is almost always funny? Most of us enjoy being around people like this because they encourage us to laugh at the world and at ourselves.

1. In groups, answer the following questions.

   ■ Who is your favorite comedian, in the movies or on TV, or favorite humorous person that you know?

   ■ What is so funny about this person?

   ■ How can a joke be delivered effectively? Ineffectively

2. Come to class prepared to tell two jokes that you think are very funny. You might want to try them out on some of your friends before telling them in class.

Charlie Chaplin, a comic actor with universal appeal.

4 **Including Humor in Conversations.** Divide into small groups. Your teacher will assign a topic and ask you to talk together for ten minutes. Possible topics include school, work, sports, dating, marriage, children, politics, or television. As often as possible, include a joke or folk saying in your conversation. When the time is up, share your group's best jokes and sayings with the rest of the class.

PART 4 # Focus on Testing

Listen to the two conversations. After each conversation, you will hear a question. Circle the letter of the best answer to each question.

Conversation 1
a. because she doesn't like animals
b. because his jokes are old and silly
c. because she likes his jokes, but needs to rest now
d. because she wants to take a coffee break

Conversation 2
a. If you're not sure about saying something, don't say it.
b. Mr. Leonard might not be at the awards dinner.
c. Harold doesn't know how to tell a funny story.
d. Don't doubt yourself.

Video Activities: An Endangered Species

Before You Watch.   Answer the following questions in small groups.

1. What is a kangaroo and where are they found?

2. How do kangaroos move?
    a. They run.   b. They fly.
    c. They swim.   d. They jump.

3. Have you ever seen a kangaroo in a tree?

Watch.   Answer these questions in small groups.

1. What kind of animal is this video about?

2. How is this animal different from a normal kangaroo?

3. What helps this animal climb trees?
    a. large teeth   b. muscular tail
    c. strong legs   d. curved claws

4. Where is this animal found?

5. Scientists believe that there are _____ tree kangaroos left.
    a. many   b. no   c. few

6. What are the two threats to this animal's survival?
    a. other kangaroos   b. loss of habitat
    c. hunting by people   d. disease

Watch Again.

1. What adjectives describe tree kangaroos?
    a. dangerous   b. shy
    c. friendly   d. happy
    e. reclusive

2. Dr. Betts studies how these animals _____, _____, and _____.
    a. eat   b. reproduce
    c. live   d. behave

3. People hunt tree kangaroos for their _____.
    a. meat   b. skins
    c. claws   d. tails

4. How many new species of tree kangaroos have been found in the past decade?
    _____

After You Watch.   Discuss these questions with your class.

1. Do you know of any other animals that are endangered? What are they?

2. Do you think that it is important to save endangered animals? Why or why not?

Appendix

Appendix 1

Chapter 1 Part 3 Talk It Over

1. Zero, because 0 times *anything* is 0.
2. The answer will be 111,111,111 no matter which digit is used.
3. Mary is only five years old and cannot reach the button for the 12th floor.
4. None. Hens can't talk.
5. The letter *m*.
6. Just divide the answer by 4 and you will have the number your partner started with.
7. a. The man first takes the sheep across the river and leaves it there.
    b. He then returns and takes the lion across the river.
    c. He leaves the lion on the other side and takes the sheep back to the first side.
    d. Then he takes the hay over to the other side and leaves the hay there with the lion.
    e. Finally, he returns for the sheep and the job is done.
8. One. To get the answer, you must draw a family tree. In the tree shown here, the governor is A, his wife is a, and his guest is D.

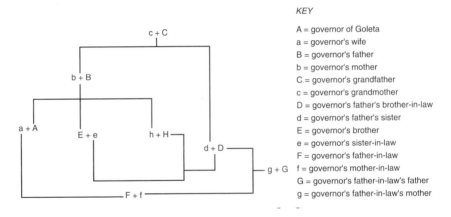

KEY

A = governor of Goleta
a = governor's wife
B = governor's father
b = governor's mother
C = governor's grandfather
c = governor's grandmother
D = governor's father's brother-in-law
d = governor's father's sister
E = governor's brother
e = governor's sister-in-law
F = governor's father-in-law
f = governor's mother-in-law
G = governor's father-in-law's father
g = governor's father-in-law's mother

Chapter 6 Part 1 Activity 3 Crossword Puzzle

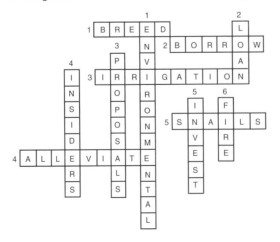

Tapescript

Chapter 1 New Challenges

PART 2 Listening to Make Predictions

Lecture: Learning to Speak Someone Else's Language

Professor:	Good morning! I am James Munro, and this is Linguistics 101.
Students:	Good morning. Hello. Hi.
Professor:	Our topic today is "Learning to Speak Someone Else's Language." Before I begin, I'd like to hear your questions on the topic. What does the title "Learning to Speak Someone Else's Language" bring to mind? What does it make you think about? Just call out your questions.
Student 1:	What is language? I mean, where does it come from?
Professor:	Good question. Any others?
Student 2:	Who uses language? Is it only humans?
Professor:	Interesting. Next.
Student 3:	When does language develop? At what age?
Professor:	Good, got that. Yes, go ahead.
Student 4:	How many languages are there in the world? And can we ever really learn to speak someone else's language?
Professor:	Hmm. Any more? No? Then let's begin with that last question. Can we ever really learn to speak another person's language? Well, I think that we must at least try. You see, language is the only window we have to see into someone else's mind. But this presents us with a paradox. On the one hand, language helps us communicate with each other. On the other hand, communication is not possible when we don't understand the words and symbols that someone else is using. OK so far?
	Communication can fail even when two people have the same native language. You see, in addition to their usual agreed-upon meanings, words and concepts have very personal meanings for each person based on memories and experiences. Does that make sense to you?
Student 2:	I think so. Is it like when I hear the word "dog," I might think of the little beagle named Sarge that I had when I was a kid, but my friend, who is afraid of dogs, might think of Cujo? You know, that huge dog that attacked people in that old Steven King movie?
Professor:	That's right! Exactly! Here's another example: A rose may be just a beautiful object to me, but it may remind you of a lovely summer in England or a romantic birthday present. So you can see the problem, right?
Students:	Sure. Right. Uh-huh.
Professor:	Also, there are between 3,000 and 6,000 public languages in the world and we must add approximately 5 billion private languages

since each of us necessarily has one. Did you get that? With this many languages, it's amazing that we understand each other at all.

However, sometimes we do communicate successfully. We do learn to speak other languages. But learning to speak a language seems to be a very mysterious process. Now this brings us back to the first question on our list: Where does language come from? And how does it develop?

For a long time, people thought that we learned language only by imitation and association. For example, a baby touches a hot pot and starts to cry. The mother says, "Hot, hot!" and the baby - when it stops crying - imitates the mother and says, "Hot, hot." The baby then associates the word "hot" with the burning feeling. However, Noam Chomsky, a famous linguist, said that although children do learn some words by imitation and association, they also combine words to make sentences in ways they have never heard before. Chomsky suggested that this accomplishment is possible because human babies have an innate ability to learn any language in the world. Are you following me?

Student 5: Maybe.

Professor: Chomsky says that children are born with the ability to learn language, but this does not explain how children begin to use language in different ways. For example, as children develop their language skills, they quickly learn that language is used for more than stating facts such as "The girl is tall." They learn to make requests, to give commands, to agree, to disagree, to explain, to excuse, and even to lie. The uses of language seem endless. This is the positive side of the paradox. Did you get that?

Students: Maybe. Not exactly. I'm not sure.

Professor: In other words, language is a wonderful way of communicating our ideas to other people. The negative side of the paradox is that not all people speak the same language, and therefore we cannot understand each other.

So we're back to where we started. Can we ever really learn to speak someone else's language?

For now, let's assume that we can learn to speak someone else's language, not just a few polite phrases, but really learn to speak it fluently. We know that we will be able to communicate with other people who speak that language. But something else happens as well. I think that learning another language can transform us as individuals—it can change our worldview and even our personalities. For example, if we speak French fluently, we can begin to see the world in a way that is typically French. That is, we can view the world from an entirely different point of view, which might change our personalities dramatically. Are you following me?

Student 3: Not exactly. Professor Munro, I'm not sure that I buy the idea that I would actually become someone else just because I learned to speak another language.

Professor:	Okay, consider this. A linguist named Benjamin Lee Whorf said that our native language actually determines the way we see the world. I believe he meant something like this: Imagine a language that has no words for anger, fear, or jealousy. Does that mean that we won't experience these emotions if we are native speakers of that language? Or, imagine a language that has twenty-five words for love. Will we be able to love more deeply if we are native speakers of that language?
Student 3:	Well, maybe. But I think there's a problem with this point of view.
Professor:	Okay. What do you think that might be?
Student 3:	Well, for one thing, that point of view ignores the fact that languages change and that they borrow words from other languages. For example, English sometimes uses words from other languages to express a thought or name a thing in a better way.
Professor:	Yes, of course! As I sat at home preparing for this lecture, I looked up at the collage on my wall and took a bite out of my croissant. Later I experienced a moment of déjà-vu. So, to describe my activities this morning, I have just used three words borrowed from French—collage, croissant, and déjà-vu — because they describe certain things and experiences better than any English words.
Student 3:	So English is transformed by words from other languages that express things that really cannot be expressed very well in English?
Professor:	Right! In a way, this transformation is what happens to us when we learn to speak someone else's language. We learn, perhaps, to express things that could not be expressed as well—or even at all—in our own languages. We may also learn to understand things in ways that we could not before. Does that make sense to you? We can begin to experience what it must be like to be born into another culture.
	Oh, my. Our time seems to be up. Next time, be prepared to talk about your own experiences in learning about another culture as you learned to speak a second language. Also, please read Chapters 1 and 2 in your textbook and think about this question: If we learn one language so easily as children, why is it such a challenge to learn a second language as adults?

PART 3   ## Offering and Requesting Clarification

1   **Listening for Intonation.   Page 11.**

Conversation 1
Ms. Garcia is talking to a group of employees.

Ms. Garcia:	To figure out the daily costs, you'll have to add up all the numbers in column A, divide by 30, and then multiply by the number of days you'll be there. Is that clear?

Question 1: Which of the expressions from the explaination box does Ms. Garcia use?
Question 2: What is her intention when she uses this expression?

Conversation 2
Mrs. Smith is talking to her son.

> *Mrs. Smith:* No, you can't watch TV. First you have to clean up your room, write a thank-you note to your grandmother for your birthday present, put your bicycle away, take your model airplane project off the kitchen table, put your library books in the car so we can return them tomorrow, finish your homework, and take out the garbage. Is that clear?

Question: Mrs. Smith uses the same expression that Ms. Garcia did in Conversation 1. What is Mrs. Smith's intention when she uses this expression?

PART 4	# Focus on Testing. Page 15.

Listen to the two speakers. After each speaker finishes talking, you will hear a question. Circle the letter of the best answer to each question.

Speaker 1
Male college student: Excuse me, Dr. Jackson. I didn't get that last part. Did you just say that a pun was a kind of play on words?

Question: What does the speaker want to know?

Speaker 2
Female professor: In different parts of the world, some languages are dying out. In these places, children don't learn to speak their parents' native language. So, as the parents die, their language dies too.

Question: What is the speaker's main point?

Chapter 2	## Looking at Learning

PART 2	## Listening for Main Ideas

Lecture: Learning to Listen/ Listening to Learn

Lilia: Hello. Welcome to the first freshman study-skills class of the semester. I'm Lilia Rothman. I'm a senior in the Education Department and I'll be the TA for this course. Has everyone found a place to sit? There's a chair down here, if you need one.

Okay. Let's get started. Did you know that people spend more than half the time they are awake communicating? They are either writing, reading, speaking, or listening. Which do you think people do most? Which do you think they do least?

Well, people seem to spend the most amount of time listening and the least writing. Did you guess that? Here's an example: A sales manager for the electronics division of Sylvania Electric Products kept a record of his day and he found that he spent 70 or 80 percent of his day on the telephone. One-half of that time was spent listening.

Reading and listening are similar because they're both ways we receive messages. Yet reading and listening are very different in three important ways. First of all, we can reread something, but usually we cannot "re-listen." Unless we have a tape recorder, we cannot hear the message again. And what we listen to is not usually written down. The second difference is control of the speed of the message. We can control the speed of the message when we read, but not when we listen. When we listen, the speed of the message is established by the speaker. And third, we must understand the meaning of words and ideas immediately when listening. You can't use a dictionary very easily while you're listening.

Now, how fast do people speak and how fast do they listen? People speak English at a rate of about 125 words per minute, but people can listen much more quickly than this. Actually, people can listen at a rate of 300 words per minute and not lose any comprehension. So it's easy to stop listening for a while, think about your lunch, your upcoming basketball game, or your boyfriend or girlfriend, and then listen again without losing the gist of what is being said.

But good listeners aren't thinking about their lunch, their basketball game, or their boyfriends or girlfriends—unless, of course, they are listening *to* their boyfriends or girlfriends. Good listeners do three important things to focus their attention while listening and to keep their minds from wandering.

First, good listeners think ahead of the speaker and try to predict, or guess, what will be said. For example, in a basic science course you may know that the lecturer will follow the textbook. So you say to yourself, "Now he's going to talk about Newton's ideas from Chapter 2 because he's already talked about Galileo from Chapter 1." Second, good listeners evaluate what the speaker says. They say to themselves, "That doesn't seem logical," "I can think of a counterexample," or "That must be right; I can think of two more examples." And finally, good listeners review in their minds what was said.

Now, when you're out there in those big lecture classes, you can do more than just listen and follow the three guidelines for good listening. You can take notes. When you take notes, you're focused. You are less likely to daydream. If you take notes, it's easier to review the material in the lecture. And later you may find material and ideas in your notes that you have forgotten since the lecture.

When you take notes, there are two techniques to keep in mind to make your notes more valuable. The first technique is to keep your notes clear and brief. Write in short, uncomplicated sentences. For example, if the lecture is on birds and the lecturer says, "The smallest bird alive is that tiny but beautiful hummingbird from Cuba called the bee hummingbird, which is about $2\frac{1}{2}$ inches long," then you might write only "Bee hummingbird is $2\frac{1}{2}$ inches." The second technique is to make a schedule for reviewing notes. For example, you may decide to review your notes every night after dinner. Or you may decide to do it just before you go to sleep or the first thing in the morning. But once you decide, you should stay on schedule.

So . . . on to note taking. There are two basic systems for note taking: the thesis/conclusion system and the fact/principle system. The thesis/conclusion system works best with well-organized lectures that have an introduction, a body, and a conclusion. The fact/principle system works best with less-organized lectures. With these lectures you can write the facts on one side of the page, draw a line down the middle, and write the principles on the other side of the page. Then. when you review, you can see if the principles tie together into one main concept or thesis.

Okay let's sum up—does anyone remember the three rules for good listening?

Kim: Um, think ahead of the speaker?

Lilia: Yeah, think ahead of the speaker and try to predict what's coming next. That's one. Who's got another one? Kim?

Kim: Evaluate what is being said. You know, decide if it makes sense or not.

Lilia: Right. That's two. Who knows the third rule for good listening? Okay, Kim, go for it. Give us the third one, too.

Kim: I think it's that you should always review what has been said. Maybe say it in your own words in your head.

Lilia: Yes, right! And Kim wins the prize for good listening. Now who remembers the two techniques for note taking that I talked about?

Kazu: Keep your notes short and on the main point.

Lilia: Right, Kazu. Keep notes brief and to the point. And the second technique?

Bill: Always make time to review your notes. You know, make a schedule and stick to it.

Lilia: Great, Bill! Okay, that's two more good listeners. And last but not least, what are the two systems of note taking that I presented tonight? What? No one took notes on this? Well, get out some paper now and write this down. The two systems of note taking are:

1. The thesis/conclusion system
2. The fact/principle system

Great! I can see that you're all setting up your notes in just the right way. And believe me, you'll get plenty of chances to practice this term

Well, that's it for tonight. Review your notes, and I'll see you next time.

Asking for Confirmation

1 Listening for Appropriate Expressions and Intonation. Page 24.

Conversation 1

At the side of the road, a lost driver is asking a police officer for directions.

Driver: Pardon me. How do I get to the University Library?

Police Officer: You make a U-turn, go back on Washington until you hit Jefferson, then make a right turn, and it's the second white building on your left.

Driver: Could you repeat that, please?

Police Officer: Sure. You make a U-turn, go back on Washington until you hit Jefferson, about three blocks, then make a right turn, and it's the second white building on your left.

Driver: You mean I turn around and stay on Washington until I get to Jefferson and then make a right?

Police Officer: Yeah, that's right.

Driver: And did you say it's a white building on the left?

Police Officer: Uh-huh.

Driver: Thanks a lot.

Police Officer: You're welcome.

Question: Did the lost driver ask for confirmation appropriately?

Conversation 2

Here is a conversation between a professor and a student.

Student: I didn't get the directions on the test. That's why I didn't do well.

Instructor: Well, Tim, the directions say "Answer IA and then choose and answer IB or IC or ID."

Student: Do you mean to say that we had to do A and B or C or D?

Instructor: Yes, you had a choice for the second half of the question.

Student: Oh, okay.

Question: Did the student respond appropriately to the instructor's explanation?

Conversation 3

Here is a similar conversation between the same professor and student.

Student: Professor Thompson, I'm not sure I understand the directions on this test.

Instructor: Well, Tim, the directions say "Answer 1 A and then choose and answer 1B or 1C or 1D."

Student: You mean that we all do 1A, but then we each could do any one of 1B, C, or D?

Instructor:	That's right, Tim.
Student:	Oh, now I see. I won't make that mistake again. Thank you.

Question 1: How do you feel about this student's confirmation strategy?
Question 2: Do your classmates feel the same way? Ask them.

Conversation 4
In this conversation, a student is talking to an administrative assistant about the pre-registration procedure.

Student:	What do I do now?
Assistant:	You take that white sheet and the blue card. You fill out the white sheet with the courses you want. Then you have your advisor sign the white sheet and the blue card, and you turn them in to the first-floor office in Building Four and pay your fees.
Student:	You mean I've got to have my advisor sign both the sheet and the card, and then I've got to stand in line again?

Question: How would you react if you were this administrative assistant?

Conversation 5
Here is another conversation between an administrative assistant and a student.

Student:	Excuse me, could you tell me what I must do next to preregister?
Assistant:	You take that white sheet and the blue card. You fill out the white sheet with the courses you want. Then you have your advisor sign the white sheet and the blue card, and you turn them in to the first-floor office in Building Four and pay your fees.
Student:	I'm not sure I understand. Do you mean that the advisor must sign both forms? And that I take the forms to Building Four and pay my fees there?
Assistant:	Yes, that's right.
Student:	Oh, okay. Now I understand. Thank you.

Question: What is the main difference between Conversations 4 and 5?

PART 4 Focus on Testing. Page 27.

Listen to the two speakers. After each speaker finishes talking, you will hear a question. Circle the letter of the best answer to each question.

Speaker 1
Student:	Wow, Frank! You mean you're taking French 4, Biology 2, Intro to Economics, American Civilization, Music Appreciation, and Beginning Acting? That's a really heavy load for your first semester.

Question: What is the speaker implying?

Speaker 2

Student: I can't believe this! I'm spending over $2,000 a year for this meal plan, and it doesn't include meals on Saturday and Sunday!

Question: Why is the speaker unhappy?

Chapter 3 Relationships

Listening for Straw Man Arguments

Lecture: Family Networks and the Elderly

Professor: Good morning. We've got twelve people signed up for this seminar on families and aging. I'm really glad to see so much interest in this topic.

Well, to begin, I'm going to present some statistics on the family in the United States. Then I'll introduce four assumptions some people make about families in the United States based on those statistics. Finally, I'm going to present some cross-cultural data, facts, and statistics on the elderly from research done back in the sixties. I haven't found any studies on this topic more recent than that. Maybe one of you will do a research project on this topic and present more recent cross-cultural data. Okay?

Students: Great. Sure. Sounds good.

Professor: Good. First of all, let's define the elderly. How old do you have to be to be considered elderly?

Student 1: 75?

Student 2: 65?

Student 3: 70?

Professor: Well, the elderly are generally defined as people over 65. But now that people are living and working much longer, that age is closer to 75. Let me tell you some interesting facts and statistics about family patterns in the United States. These statistics are often reported in magazines or newspapers to show that family life in the United States is not very good. Let's take a closer look at these statistics.

The first fact that is often reported is that Americans move a great deal. Believe it or not, about 18% of American households moved last year.

Second, since the beginning of the twentieth century, there has been a decline in the average size of households and a dramatic increase in the percentage of one person households—that means people living alone.

Third, today in the United States one in every two marriages ends in divorce – that's 50%.

And fourth, you may be surprised to find that over 60% of the children born in 1997 will spend some time in single-parent house-

	holds by the time they are 18. That's nearly two out of every three children.
Student 1:	I'm surprised that it isn't higher.
Professor:	Higher?
Student 1:	Yes. I mean, I don't know very many people whose parents are still married.
Professor:	Well, your perception of American lifestyles is based on what you've observed. And these statistics *do* indicate that there have been changes in lifestyles in this century. But looking at these changes has led some people to make assumptions about the elderly and how they might feel isolated in the United States. Let's consider three assumptions based on these changes, and then let's look at the research to decide whether they are true or false.

The first assumption is that since Americans move a great deal, the elderly typically live far away from their children.

The second assumption is that because most Americans live in small households and do not live in extended families, the elderly hardly ever see their relatives, including their siblings.

And the third assumption is that because of the high number of divorces and single-parent homes, the American family is disjointed and the elderly rarely see their children.

All three assumptions would lead you to believe that in the United States, the elderly might feel isolated. But is there any truth to these assumptions about the elderly and their families? Is there any data— any statistics—that can really support this thinking? |
| *Student 2:* | It seems logical. |
| *Professor:* | Well, it may seem logical, but let's look at these three beliefs- these assumptions- again and see just how true they are according to research that was begun in the sixties. Let's see if the data- the statistics- from this research supports them. This research was done by Ethel Shanas at the University of Illinois, Chicago Circle.

Let's look at the first assumption. It says that because Americans move so often, the elderly typically live very far from their children. Well, let's see if this is true. Shanas found that in the United States, 60% of the elderly live with their children or within ten minutes of their children. Shanas's study also included some European countries, and on your handout, you can see that more elderly people in the United States live with their children or within ten minutes of their children than in Denmark. However, it is interesting to note that for the most part, the elderly in the United States interviewed for another recent survey preferred to live in their own homes or apartments rather than with their children. |
| *Student 3:* | So the first assumption is not true. |
| *Professor:* | Right. Now let's look at the second assumption that because people do not live in extended families, the elderly hardly ever see their siblings—brothers and sisters—or other relatives. As you can see on the handout, 41% of women and 34% of men had seen a sibling within the past week. |

Student 1:	So the second assumption is not true either.
Professor:	Exactly. So how about the third assumption that because of the high number of divorces and single-parent homes, the American family is disjointed and the elderly rarely see their children. Look at Table 2 on the handout. You can see that over 50% of the elderly had seen their children that day or the day before. In any case, 78% of the elderly had seen their children within the last week. Also on the handout, you can see how the United States compares with some other European countries.
Student 2:	The third assumption is not even close to being true.
Professor:	I agree. Now, let's review what we have learned today about the elderly. First, the truth is that most of the elderly do not live far from their children. Second, the elderly do see their siblings and other relatives fairly frequently. And third, by and large, the elderly do see their children. Since this data indicates that the elderly actually do spend quite a bit of time with their families, they probably do not feel isolated. So from my point of view, we can, in general, feel good about how the elderly are treated in the United States.
Student 3:	At least according to the statistics from Shanas's study in the sixties!
Professor:	Yes, Molly. And that's why I thought it would be a good idea for students in this class to do a research project and get more recent data. What do you think we'll find? Do you think things have changed in the last 20 to 30 years? Do you think these assumptions are still false, or might they be true now? Let's take a break, and then we'll begin to develop our research plan.

PART 4 Focus on Testing. Page 38.

Listen to the two speakers. After each speaker finishes talking, you will hear a question. Circle the letter of the best answer to each question.

Speaker 1

Mother:	OK kids, listen up. Normally we divide up the housework, but this week Dad has to help Grandpa and Grandma paint their house. So, James and Ruth, you're both going to have to pitch in more around here.

Question: What is the speaker's main point?

Speaker 2

Father:	We hardly ever take the dog on our summer vacation, but she's getting so old and looks so sad when we leave her. I can't bear to think of her in a kennel again. You think she'll like the Grand Canyon?

Question: What is the father trying to say to the family?

Chapter 4 ▮ Health and Leisure

Study Session: What Makes Us Tick: The Cardiac Muscle

Tory: So what are we studying next?

Susan: Let's go over the notes from Professor Miller's lecture.

Tory: You mean the lecture on the heart?

Susan: Uh-huh.

Fred: Great idea. Why don't we go through the notes and make sure we understand everything?

Susan: Sure.

Tory: OK. Let me just get my notes out. Ready.

Susan: Well, first she said that it was certainly the action of the cardiac muscles that makes such a small organ as the heart incredibly efficient. And then she talked about how the shape of the heart is similar to a pear. I don't exactly understand that analogy.

Fred: Well, think of the pictures Professor Miller showed us. In my opinion, it *did* look like a pear, right side up, with the widest part at the bottom, leaning a little to the right.

Susan: Yeah, I get it now. OK, let's talk about the parts. It's got four hollow chambers—two in the top part and two in the bottom part. And what did she say about the walls of the heart?

Fred: She said that they're fairly thick, approximately like a slice of bread, at the bottom. And at the top, they're thinner, about as thin as an orange peel.

Susan: Are you sure about that? I'm fairly certain that it was the other way around.

Tory: No, I'm positive that Fred is right. I have it here in my notes.

Susan: OK. Now what else? Oh, yeah . . . The strips of muscle at the bottom of the heart are like string around a hollow ball. How's that for an analogy?

Fred: That's good.

Susan: You know, I was surprised that the heart is so small. It's only slightly larger than a tightly closed fist. I like how Professor Miller had us each make a fist and look at it so we could see that it was about the same size as a heart.

Tory: Then remember how she told us to open and close our hands? She wanted us to see how the muscles contract and relax over and over again our whole lives.

Fred: Yup. That's the heartbeat. Contraction and relaxation—very regular and even – the beat is just like the tick tock of a clock.

Susan: But didn't she say that the rate can vary?

Fred:	Yeah ... In general, the rate of the heartbeat varies in relation to the size of the person or animal. An elephant's heart averages about 25 beats per minute. A small bird's heart averages about 1,000 beats per minute. The heart of a human infant at birth beats about 130 times a minute. In a small child, it beats about 90 to 100 times a minute. The average adult rate for men is about 75 beats per minute. And the rate for women averages about 7 to 8 beats faster per minute than the rate for men. Why is that?
Tory:	I think she said that's because women are smaller than men, but I don't really understand why that is, do you guys?
Fred, Susan:	No, not really. Let's ask her in class.
Tory:	Okay. Hmm ... Anyway, I think it's pretty amazing that this adds up to about 100,000 heartbeats a day for an adult male. That's about 2,600,000,000 heartbeats in a lifetime.
Fred, Susan:	Wow!
Tory:	Yeah, and another amazing thing is that the heart doesn't have any nerves in it. So, no messages are sent from the brain through the nerves to the cardiac muscles. The brain doesn't tell the cardiac muscles to beat. Nothing does.
Fred:	So that means that the heartbeat starts in the cardiac muscle itself?
Susan:	That's right. It's different from the other muscles and organs in that way.
Fred:	Oh yeah. Remember what Professor Miller said about how a very small piece of cardiac muscle can be kept alive in a dish with special liquid in it? And that the muscle will continue to beat all by itself!
Tory:	Uh-huh. Scientists don't really understand how the cardiac muscle does this yet, but I bet that they will in 10 or 15 years.
Fred:	OK, but how does the heart work with all of the other organs?
Tory:	Well, the heart is similar to a pump. Basically, it pumps blood to the rest of the body. Let's see, I've got it here in my notes. The heart pumps approximately 5 quarts of blood a minute if you are resting and 35 quarts of blood a minute if you are exercising. That's 4,500 gallons a day and 40,951,000 gallons—or 150,000,000 liters—of blood in a lifetime! Can you believe that the heart works that hard?
Fred:	Don't look so worried, Tory. I'm pretty sure your heart isn't going to quit yet.
Susan:	Right. Remember . . . Professor Miller said that the heart rests a lot too. In fact, a heartbeat takes eight-tenths of a second, and half of that time the heart rests.
Fred:	Yeah—I'd say you're going to be around for a good long time!

Expressing Opinions

1 **Recognizing a Know-It-All. Page 47.**

Conversation 1
Listen to the debate between Joe and Paul.

Joe: I suspect that heart disease is the number one killer in the United States.

Paul: No, no! It's cancer.

Joe: Well, I'm almost positive that it's heart disease. Didn't Dr. Strong say that ...

Paul: Nope. You're wrong. It's cancer.

Question 1: Does Joe express an opinion?
Question 2: Does Paul express an opinion?
Question 3: Does Paul indicate that his is a personal opinion?
Question 4: Which person sounds like a "know-it-all"? Why?

Conversation 2
Now listen to another version of Joe and Paul's debate.

Joe: I suspect that heart disease is the number one killer in the United States.

Paul: Oh, I always thought it was cancer.

Joe: Well, I'm almost positive that it's heart disease. Didn't Dr. Strong say that ...

Paul: Yes, and not everyone will agree with me, but I'm pretty sure Dr. Strong doesn't have his facts straight.

Question: What expressions does Paul use to introduce his personal opinions this time?

PART 4 **Focus on Testing. Page 49.**

Listen to the two speakers. After each speaker finishes talking, you will hear a question. Circle the letter of the best answer to each question.

Speaker 1
Man: Personally, I don't think that anyone should smoke and I'm positive that smoking causes cancer. Of course, not everyone will agree with me, but I don't think we should make laws about what people can and can't do in restaurants and bars.

Question: What is the speaker implying?

Speaker 2

Woman: I should lose some weight. I read in the newspaper that most Americans are eight to sixteen pounds overweight, and I'm pretty sure that I'm part of this majority.

Question: What does the speaker think?

Chapter 5 High Tech, Low Tech

PART 2 Taking Notes on a Field Trip

Field Trip Demonstration: Space Flight: A Simulation

Guide: Hello. We'd like to welcome Professor Chapman and his aeronautics class to Houston, Texas, and the Lyndon B. Johnson Space Center. Today, without leaving the ground, we are going to experience the excitement of a flight into space.

We are now seated in the space center's amphitheater. The screen in front of you shows the inside of the space shuttle orbiter. The advanced technology used in this presentation will simulate for you what it is like to be a crew member at work on an actual space mission. Our mission today is to capture and repair a $75 million solar observation satellite that has been in orbit since 1980.

Okay. Fasten your seatbelts and we will begin our simulated flight on the spaceship *Enterprise*.

All right? Now, imagine we have been inside the orbiter for about two hours making sure everything is ready.

Mission Control: This is Mission Control. It is now T minus 3.8 seconds.

Guide: T stands for takeoff, of course. And we hear the three engines fire.

Mission Control: T minus 1 second. T minus zero.

Guide: At T minus zero the two booster rockets fire, and three seconds later we are lifted off the ground by the combined energy of the five engines.

Through the window we see the tower disappear. We feel the effects of acceleration on our bodies as our spaceship speeds up to four times the speed of sound (which is about eleven hundred feet per second in the air) and revolves one hundred and twenty degrees. We are now turned upside down with our heads toward the ground as we climb in the air and go out over the ocean. How do you like the feeling? We won't be right side up until we are in orbit.

Two minutes after takeoff, the fuel in the booster rockets has been used up. They drop away as we continue gaining speed. Six minutes later we have reached 15 times the speed of sound and the graceful spaceship is flying free, heading into orbit around the earth at a height of 690 miles.

Once we reach full altitude we change our program on the computer. This shuts down the main engines, and we can now control the orbiter's movement with small bursts of rocket fire from engines in the nose and tail. Put your hand on the control stick. Move the control stick to the right and we will roll. Although we don't feel it without gravity, you can see the motion through the window. If you move your wrist on the control forward or backward, we will go up or down. A twist makes us go to the right or left.

Let's have a few of you take turns with this, so you can get the full effect.

Student 1: My turn? OK. Here we go. Lean left!

Student 2: OK, now I'll straighten us up.

Student 3: Anyone for a complete roll?

All Students: Enough! Enough! I'm getting dizzy!

Guide: OK. Let's get ready for the next phase of your mission.

Look through the window. The cargo doors are opening. These doors open when we arrive in orbit and remain open to provide the ship with necessary ventilation throughout our stay in space. As I said before, the purpose of this mission is to repair a $75 million solar observation satellite that has been in orbit since 1980. Since the failure of its control system, the satellite has been moving through space without guidance—moving so fast that it cannot be reached directly by the Remote Manipulation Arm, which we'll call the RMA.

The RMA is a 50-foot mechanical arm attached to the outside of the orbiter. Look at the handout we gave you as you came into the amphitheater. From the drawing, you can see that the mechanical arm is very much like your own arm. The arm is attached to the orbiter at the shoulder, and an elbow and a wrist allow the arm to move and bring satellites into the cargo bay. This maneuver is necessary in order to repair the satellite. There are television cameras at both the elbow and wrist so we can see what's going on. The hand, or what is called the *end effector*, is fitted with three inside wires. A short arm of the satellite is caught by these wires.

If you look out the window, you will see two astronauts in space suits outside. They are going to slow down the satellite manually so we can connect it to the RMA from here inside. Remember, we said that the satellite was moving too quickly to be picked up directly by the RMA.

Student 1: Wow, Look at that!

Student 2: Yeah, they're actually grabbing the satellite with their hands!

Guide: Now it's our turn. The astronauts outside have captured the satellite for us and now we have to get to work. We must manipulate the arm, bending its wrist, elbow, and shoulder joints to lower the damaged satellite into our cargo bay.

Great job! Okay, now let's wait while the astronauts repair the satellite in the cargo bay. It should only take a few moments. Just a small part on the outside of it needs to be replaced. Uh, huh, they almost have the old part off. That's it. Now they're putting the new part in place. And tightening it down. There! I think they've got it!

Mission Control: *Enterprise*, this is Mission Control. Congratulations! Your mission has been accomplished. Now prepare for reentry.

Guide: OK, crew, let's get ready for reentry by closing the cargo bay doors. We fire our engines to slow the orbiter so that it begins to fall toward earth. We enter the atmosphere at an altitude of 400,000 feet. We are now 5,000 miles from our landing site. The friction of air causes us to slow down from our entry speed of 16,000 miles per hour, but it also causes us to heat up. However, we are protected from surface temperatures of 2,750 degrees Fahrenheit by the thermal tiles covering the ship. The heat is so great that our radio communications are cut off for 12 minutes on our descent. Our onboard computers maintain control.

As the atmosphere gets heavier, our craft changes from a spaceship into a glider. The engines shut off as we continue our descent in silence. The ground is coming up at us fast at 10,000 feet per minute, seven times faster than it would in the landing of an airplane. At just 1,500 feet our stomachs feel funny as the pilot pulls up the nose of the spaceship to slow us down. We hear the landing gear open and lock, and very quickly, we touch back down on Mother Earth and come to a stop.

The flight is over. Mission accomplished! Thanks for coming aboard the *Enterprise*. See you next time on our sister ship *Discovery*.

PART 3 Shifting Between Active and Passive Voice

1 **Contrasting the Passive and Active Voice.** **Page 58.**

Conversation 1
A school nurse and a teacher are talking about Mathew, a young student. Mathew is crying.

Teacher: Hi, Susan. Can you check out a small problem for me?
Nurse: Sure. Oh, why is Mathew crying?
Teacher: I think he and his friend Jay had a fight.
Nurse: There is a red mark on his arm.
Teacher: Oh, no! Jay must have hit him!

Conversation 2
The school nurse is telling Mathew's parents what happened.

Nurse: Hello. This is the school nurse. Is this Mathew's father?
Father: Yes it is. Is there a problem?

Nurse:	Just a small one. It seems that Mathew and his friend Jay have had a fight.
Father:	What? Was anyone hurt?
Nurse:	Yes, Mathew was hit by Jay, and he has a large mark on his arm.

Question 1: Which conversation (1 or 2) contains the passive voice?
Question 2: Why do you think the passive voice was used in this situation?

Conversation 3
A husband and wife are in the living room talking.

Husband:	What happened?
Wife:	The lights just went out!
Husband:	What do you suppose is the reason?
Wife:	They probably turned off our electricity because we didn't pay our bill.

Conversation 4
A woman is on the phone with an electric company employee.

Electric company official:	Good morning. This is Madison Electric.
Customer:	My name is Ellen Bates and my electricity went out last night.
Electric company official:	Just a minute, Mrs. Bates. I'll check your records.
Customer:	Thank you.
Electric company official:	Ah, yes, here they are.
Customer:	What happened?
Electric company official:	Your electricity has been turned off because your bill hasn't been paid.

Question 1: Which conversation (3 or 4) contains the passive voice?
Question 2: Why do you think the passive voice was used in this situation?

PART 4   # Focus on Testing. Page 61.

Listen to the two speakers. After each speaker finishes talking, you will hear a question. Circle the letter of the best answer to each question.

Speaker 1
| Woman: | Yeah, the airport was hit, too. The Weather Service says that all flights have been canceled until further notice. |

Question: What has happened at the airport?

Speaker 2

Man: Due to technical difficulties the orbiter liftoff for today has been canceled. We'll let you know when repairs are completed and it's been rescheduled.

Question: What is the speaker explaining?

Chapter 6 | Money Matters

PART 2 | ## Listening for Pros and Cons (Arguments For and Against)

Radio Program: The World Bank under Fire

Michelle Barney: Good afternoon. This is Radio K-I-Z-Z, your "total talk" radio station. I am Michelle Barney, financial reporter for Radio KIZZ, and I will be your host for today's program, "The World Bank under Fire."

I'm sure you are all aware that most of the world's population lives in developing and semi-industrialized countries. These countries do not have enough money to invest in schools, utilities, factories, and highways. One way these countries can get money is by borrowing money from an organization called the World Bank.

In 1989 the World Bank loaned about $15 billion to developing countries. By 1999, the World Bank had almost doubled this amount and loaned about $29 billion to developing nations. In theory, this huge sum of money should be helping the world's poor. Since the establishment of the World Bank in 1944, most people have assumed that these loans could only do good things for a country. But it turns out that money isn't everything.

For example, many people question the value of a dam built with World Bank money in Ethiopia. That dam destroyed the homes and lives of more people than it served with electric power. That dam also destroyed forests and endangered animals and plants. The critics of the World Bank say that this kind of help to developing countries is wasteful, destructive, and unfair. They wonder who is profiting from projects such as this one—the people or large international corporations?

Today we have a spokesperson here with us from the World Bank, Mr. George Cruz. Mr. Cruz has been with the bank for ten years and is part of a team that has been examining the effectiveness of World Bank projects. This World Bank team of insiders is coming to the same conclusions as many critics of the World Bank. They have concluded that many of the projects in the past have been economic failures and serious threats to both the environment and human rights. Mr. Cruz . . .

George Cruz:	Well, Ms. Barney, I am very happy to be here today to clarify some things about the World Bank. While much of what you say is true, I think we need to talk about the successes of the World Bank as well as the failures. We also need to talk about the positive changes the World Bank has made in its goals for the 21st century.
	But to begin, I'd like to give a brief overview of the World Bank and how it works.
Ms. Barney:	Of course. I think that would be very helpful for our listeners.
Mr. Cruz:	Now, what we call the World Bank is actually an umbrella term, a general term, for five separate organizations with five slightly different purposes. But the International Bank for Reconstruction and Development is generally what most people think of as the World Bank. In order to borrow money from this branch of the World Bank, a country must be a member. Of course, the money is supposed to be paid back with interest, as with any bank loan.
Ms. Barney:	Yes. I guess that's true, but many countries are never able to pay back the loans.
Mr. Cruz:	Yes, that has sometimes been a problem in the past, but we have a program to restructure the loans, which will alleviate that problem.
Ms. Barney:	Yes, but isn't it also true that this just means that developing countries are forced to cut spending on health, education, transportation, and welfare programs in order to reduce their huge debts to the World Bank? I've read that in some countries, the debt to the World Bank is so great that it's now the largest item in the government budgets. Furthermore, these countries have been forced to sell industries and land to foreign corporations in order to pay off debts to the World Bank.
Mr. Cruz:	Wait—Wait! One thing at a time! First, you're right that developing countries owe a lot of money to the World Bank. But the International Bank for Reconstruction and Development tries to loan money to member countries for projects that will *aid* economic development. In theory, this is good. But up to now, the bank could only loan money to buy imported goods. And to make sure that this rule was followed, the bank paid the sellers directly.
Ms. Barney:	Well, this rule is good for the countries and companies that want to sell goods to developing countries, but wouldn't this discourage local production of goods? In the long term, wouldn't this rule do more harm than good to the developing country's economy?
Mr. Cruz:	Possibly. That's one of the things we're looking at very seriously. But there are other advantages to getting a loan from this branch of the World Bank. The International Bank for Reconstruction and Development provides technical assistance along with loans. And this is a major part of our new vision for the 21st century.
	For example, Cameroon submitted a proposal for a new irrigation system along the Logone River. They hoped that with this new irrigation system, the cash income of the region would be five times greater than before. But the Bank did not approve the project right away because we know that technological advances can sometimes

cause environmental problems. Before approving the proposal, the Bank asked environmental consultants to study the project.

The consultants found that the new irrigation system would result in a serious health problem because of snails that live in the area. These snails carry a tropical disease called bilharzia.

Ms. Barney: Excuse me. Was that bilharzia with an "h"?

Mr. Cruz: Yes. Bil-har-zee-uh. Bilharzia. Anyway, the new irrigation system might have spread the snails and the disease they carried to a larger area. So the Bank paid for studies of the river system. Scientists and engineers together determined that if the irrigation system were used only when the snails were not breeding, then the disease would not spread. So, the Bank was able to solve the problem.

Ms. Barney: Yes, I understand what you mean, but wasn't there a problem getting local residents to use the system appropriately? I believe I read that some people were never convinced that the snail disease had really been taken care of, so they would not use the irrigation system at all. And another group of people never believed there was a problem in the first place, so they would not stop using the irrigation system when the snails were breeding.

Mr. Cruz: Yes, that's true. The International Bank for Reconstruction and Development is beginning to see that understanding local needs and culture may be more important than anything else in the success of a project.

Well, let me continue. The second organization under the World Bank umbrella is the International Development Association, or IDA. The IDA has approximately 160 members and makes loans that are interest free. This, of course, is good for needy countries because it allows even the poorest country to begin projects immediately. On the other hand, because little or no interest is paid, the IDA is very dependent upon contributions from member nations to support various projects.

Ms. Barney: So this is how contributing nations can dictate what governmental policies must be in place before loans will be given, right?

Mr. Cruz: Yes, exactly. Our major goal for the 21st century is to help people to help themselves, not only by providing money, but also by sharing knowledge and forming partnerships.

So, let's move on to the third organization in the World Bank group: the International Finance Corporation, or IFC. The IFC is different from the International Bank for Reconstruction and Development and the IDA because the IFC can invest in private business and industry, while the other two organizations can only invest in government projects. This is good for the country because the government does not have to guarantee the loan and it encourages the growth of private business and industry. However, the IFC is not protected if the business fails.

Also, the IFC has no control over how a company spends its money. Some people argue that the loan is more effective if people in the region spend the money in ways they think are best, without the IFC telling them what to do. They think that people outside the region do not have a thorough understanding of complex cultural and economic regional issues.

Ms. Barney: Absolutely, but is that ever really possible? I thought that the member nations get voting rights based on the amount of money they contribute to the Bank. Doesn't that mean that the wealthier nations have the most influence on which projects will be financed?

Mr. Cruz: Ideally, of course, the loans are made to countries on the basis of economic need alone. But, we all know that it is difficult to separate economic goals from political interests in today's world.

Robert McNamara, who was secretary of defense when John F. Kennedy was president of the United States, was president of the World Bank for a time. He hoped that the World Bank would be a model of international cooperation free from political self-interests. He hoped for a world in which the superpowers would join together to provide financial support for developing nations instead of arguing among themselves.

Ms. Barney: I couldn't agree more. But whether the World Bank can really make this dream a reality is a big question.

Well, our time is up and that brings us to the end of this week's program. Our guest today was George Cruz and the topic was "The World Bank under Fire." Thank you for being with us today, Mr. Cruz.

Mr. Cruz: My pleasure.

Ms. Barney: This is Michelle Barney, your host for *World Business Topics*. Please join us next week, same time, same station, K-I-Z-Z, your "total talk" radio.

| PART 3 | # Agreeing and Disagreeing |

1 **Listening for Appropriate Uses of Expressions.**   **Page 70.**

Conversation 1
In a college classroom, a student is challenging an instructor.

Instructor: And furthermore, it is my opinion that if this small country had not received financial aid from friendly countries, the war would have been lost.

Student: You've got to be kidding! Military planning was the key.

Questions: Do you think the student is being polite or rude? Why?

Conversation 2
Now listen to a different student respond to the same instructor.

Instructor: And furthermore, it is my opinion that if this small country had not received financial aid from friendly countries, the war would have been lost.

Student: Yes, but isn't it also true that excellent military planning helped?

Questions: Do you think this student responded appropriately? Why or why not?

Conversation 3

Two students are chatting in the school cafeteria.

Roger: Hey, Paul. Looks like we're having broccoli again! The only time we have anything decent to eat is when my parents visit! Then the food is so good that my parents don't understand why I think the food is overpriced.

Paul: Yes, Roger. That's precisely the point.

Question: Paul probably doesn't have too many friends. Why do you think this might be?

Conversation 4

Let's give Paul another chance to respond to Roger a bit more appropriately.

Roger: Hey, Paul. Looks like we're having broccoli again! The only time we have anything decent to eat is when my parents visit! Then the food is so good that my parents don't understand why I think the food is overpriced.

Paul: You can say that again, Roger.

Question: Why is the expression that Paul uses this time to agree with Roger more appropriate?

Conversation 5

At a corporation meeting, two board members are discussing future plans.

First board member: It's obvious that if we don't branch into other areas, eventually the company will fail.

Second board member: I don't believe that! We must cut costs!

Questions: Do you think that these board members will reach an agreement easily? Why or why not?

Conversation 6

Now listen to two other board members in a similar conversation.

Third board member: It's obvious that if we don't branch into other areas, eventually the company will fail.

Fourth board member: That's more or less true; however, I think that by cutting our costs we can accomplish a great deal.

Question 1: How is this conversation different from the previous one?
Question 2: Do you think these board members will be able to reach an agreement more or less easily than the board members in the previous conversation?

Conversation 7

At the doctor's office, a doctor is discussing her patient, a 12-year-old boy, with his mother.

Doctor: Mrs. Franklin, your son has a variety of medical problems and it's absolutely essential that he get more exercise.

Mrs. Franklin: I knew it! He's too fat!

Question 1: Is Mrs. Franklin, the patient's mother, agreeing or disagreeing with the doctor?
Question 2: Is Mrs. Franklin responding formally or informally?

Conversation 8

Listen to the doctor and Mrs. Franklin again. This time Mrs. Franklin responds differently.

Doctor: Mrs. Franklin, your son has a variety of medical problems and it's absolutely essential that he get more exercise.

Mrs. Franklin: I couldn't agree with you more, Dr. Lewis. I've been trying to get him to play sports for years.

Question 1: Is Mrs. Franklin responding formally or informally?
Question 2: Which of the two responses do you think is more appropriate? Why?

PART 4   # Focus on Testing. Page 73.

Listen to the two speakers. After each speaker finishes talking, you will hear a question. Circle the letter of the best answer to each question.

Speaker 1

Woman: It's nice that banks are beginning to make more loans to people with low incomes. On the other hand, that money comes with a lot of strings attached.

Question: What is the speaker implying?

Speaker 2

Man: You can say that again! I couldn't agree with you more. It's definitely better to pay cash than to pay interest for years and years.

Question: What is the speaker implying?

Listening for Chronological Order

Celebrity Profile: Lance Armstrong, Uphill Racer

Hello. This is Joe Hemmings and I'm pleased to welcome you to "Celebrity Profile," the show that tells the stories of people in the news who have done remarkable things and lived remarkable lives.

Lance Armstrong races bicycles. And he's pretty good at it. He's also a husband and father. He's pretty good at those things, too. This doesn't sound very special at first, but there is much more to Lance Armstrong's story. Armstrong's win in the 1999 Tour de France bicycle race is one of the most amazing stories in sports history. He was only the second American to win this race, and the win came after he had successfully battled a very deadly form of cancer.

This battle is where our profile begins. When Armstrong found out that he had cancer in October of 1996, his whole world fell apart. He couldn't bear the thought of never racing again, never marrying, and never having children. However, Armstrong says that it was his battle with cancer that transformed his body so he could become the best uphill racer in the world, and transformed his spirit so that he could become a better team member and a committed husband and father.

By 1996, when he was only 25, Armstrong had already become an international cycling champion. He was riding high on his fame, happy in his role of the wild beer-drinking boy from Texas. He was young and undisciplined, and the sports writers called him the "Bull from Texas." He had come a long way from his small hometown of Plano, Texas. He was very poor when he left Plano in 1990, but by 1996, he was making over $1 million a year. At that time, though, he still had not won the most famous of all the races: the Tour de France.

In October of 1996, he was told that he had cancer and that he would have to endure treatments of chemotherapy to eliminate 12 tumors in his chest. Eventually, he would have surgery to remove a tumor that had also formed in his brain. Things did not look good. The doctors told him that he had only a 50% chance to live, and they did not bother to discuss the future of his bicycle-racing career.

When he first began the chemotherapy treatments, he was able to keep up with his teammates on the training rides. Eventually, however, he began to ride more and more slowly. His teammates and friends couldn't stand to see him become depressed by this, so they also rode slowly. He therefore didn't realize just how poor his health had become until one day a 50-year-old woman on a heavy mountain bike passed him as he was struggling uphill on his superlight racing bike.

Most people thought that Armstrong would never race again, but he says that it was actually the chemotherapy that gave him the body he needed to win the Tour de France. He thinks that, due to the effects of chemotherapy, he was able to lose a lot of heavy muscle that he had built up from swimming as a teenager in Texas. This gave him the opportunity to rebuild his body from scratch, completely from the beginning. This time he was careful during his training to build the kind of strong and light muscles needed to climb the mountain stages of the Tour de France. And by 1999 he was ready.

However, winning the Tour de France was not the highlight of that year for Armstrong. He and all of his fans were thrilled when his wife Kristin, whom he had married a couple of years before, gave birth to their son Luke about three months after the Tour de France, in the fall of 1999. Armstrong says that facing death helped him learn what was most important in life and that training for his comeback helped him develop the qualities needed for better relationships.

But this is not the end of this amazing story. In July of both 2000 and 2001, Armstrong proved that his win in 1999 was not a fluke by winning a second and third time. No one could deny that he was back at the top of his sport. But wait! There's more! Armstrong was asked to be on the 2000 U.S. Olympic team and while he was training, he was hit on a country road by a hit-and-run driver who did not stop to help him. His wife found him two hours later lying in the road with a broken vertebra.

But this remarkable individual could not be stopped. He didn't have time for feeling sorry for himself, and he was back on his bicycle within a few days. He even managed to win a bronze medal at the Olympic Games. This behavior is typical for Armstrong, who says:

"A slow death is not for me. I don't do anything slowly, not even breathe. I want to die when I'm 100 years old, with an American flag on my back, and the star of Texas on my helmet, after screaming down a mountain on a bicycle at 75 miles per hour. I want to cross one last finish line as my wife and ten children applaud, and then I want to lie down in a field of those famous French sunflowers and gracefully die."

Yes, this would certainly be the perfect ending to a most remarkable life. This is Joe Hemmings. Good night, and please join us next week for another edition of "Celebrity Profiles."

PART 3 **Expressing Likes and Dislikes**

---

1 **Listening for Appropriate Expressions.** **Page 82.**

Conversation 1
A man is being interviewed for a job.

Interviewer:	I'm happy to say we have quite a few remarkable people working for our company.
Applicant:	Now this is my idea of a job!
Interviewer:	Ah . . . yes . . . well, we have one Nobel Prize winner in physics and one in chemistry, and they're looking for an assistant to help them organize their notes for a book that must be completed by next month.
Applicant:	Oh, no. I can't stand that kind of pressure!
Interviewer:	Oh?

Questions: Do you think the man will get the job? Why or why not?

Conversation 2

A woman is being interviewed for a job.

Interviewer: I'm happy to say we have quite a few remarkable people working for our company.

Applicant: That's wonderful! I would look forward to the opportunity to work with them.

Interviewer: Well, we have one Nobel Prize winner in physics and one in chemistry, and they're looking for an assistant to help them organize their notes for a book that must be completed by next month..

Applicant: Well, I don't really care to be a policewoman, but if they will accept my help, I'm sure that I can help them to finish on time!

Interviewer: Well, why don't we go and meet them and see what they think?

Questions: Do you think the woman will get the job? Why or why not?

Conversation 3

Rafael and Ana are discussing what to do with their leisure time.

Rafael: Hey, want to go to the concert with me on Saturday? There's a truly remarkable cello player that has been playing since she was three years old!

Ana: Oh, no . . . I hate that kind of music.

Rafael: Oh, well, I thought you might like it.

Ana: No, I don't have time for that sort of thing.

Question 1: Does Ana enjoy concerts?
Question 2: Does she express her opinion strongly, or does she soften it?
Question 3: Do you think Rafael will ask Ana out again? Why or why not?

Conversation 4

Rafael and Joyce are discussing what to do with their leisure time.

Rafael: Hi! How about going to see that new play at the experimental theater tonight? They say the man who directed it is quite remarkable and that the lead actor is sure to win an award for her performance.

Joyce: Thanks, but I don't especially like that type of theater.

Rafael: Oh, sorry, I thought you would.

Joyce: No, I dislike it because I usually don't understand what's happening.

Question 1: Does Joyce enjoy experimental theater?
Question 2: Does she express her opinion strongly?
Question 3: Do you think Rafael will ask Joyce out again? Why or why not?

Focus on Testing. Page 85.

Listen to the two speakers. After each speaker finishes talking, you will hear a question. Circle the lettter of the best answer to each question.

Speaker 1

Man: I just don't have time for garage sales! I don't care if these things used to be owned by someone famous. What a rotten way to spend a perfectly good Sunday—looking at other people's junk. How ridiculous.

Question: What does the speaker think?

Speaker 2

Woman: I really enjoy discussing the lives of remarkable people. And I love reading. What a great idea—an all biography book list. Now that's my idea of a great class!

Question: What does the speaker think?

Chapter 8 Creativity

Listening for Signal Words

Lecture: Creativity: As Essential to the Engineer as to the Artist

Professor: Today we will continue our discussion of the creative process in general. Then we'll take up the topic of what things might inhibit this creative process in your work. This topic is applicable to any area that you may specialize in.

Well—to pick up where we left off last time- creativity is mysterious. It's one of those things we all recognize when we see it, but we do not really understand what it is or how it works. Some people seem to be naturally creative, but we don't know why they are. Is creativity an inborn gift like athletic ability, or is it something that can be acquired, like money or knowledge? Perhaps if we analyze the creative process carefully, we might get some ideas about what it is and how it might work in our lives.

The creative process has always been accepted in the arts. But creativity doesn't only play a role in the arts. Every major scientific discovery began with someone imagining the world differently from the way others saw it. And this is what creativity is all about—imagining the world in a new way. And despite what you may believe about the limits of your own creative imaginations, you do have the ability to imagine the world in an absolutely new way. In fact, everyone does! We're born with it. Cave painters in the Stone Age had it.

Musicians in the last century had it. And you have it. And what's more, you use it every day, almost every moment of your life. Your creative imagination is what you use to make sense of your experiences. It is your creative mind that gets meaning from the chaos of your experiences and brings order to your world.

Let me emphasize again that (1) everyone has creative abilities and (2) we are all creating our own realities at every moment. Let me illustrate this by having you look at the large "No Smoking" signs on the walls. Do you recognize the sign at one glance, or do you see it in parts, small sections, letter by letter? When I am being deliberately analytical, I feel I see the world in pieces. What is really going on is that the eye really does "see" things in pieces. It vibrates with great speed, taking brief, narrow pictures of the world. Then the mind combines, or fuses, those individual pictures into a larger picture—a creation. It's this creation that gives us a sense of the whole. So the mind, then, creates an interpretation of what comes in through the senses.

Now I'll explain how art is connected with this process of interpretation and ordering of the world. The artist sees a fragmentary, disordered series of events—pieces of light, color, moments in life, of conversation—and brings them together into a work of art to make the world more understandable. But art is not just an activity for professional artists. The real story is that we do the same things as the artist every day, all the time. In this way, we are artists and creators in our lives, without effort.

Now you may be wondering at this point why so many people want to be more creative if, as we said, human beings are naturally creative. I'm going to answer that by telling you that although the mind is spontaneously creative when we are very young, as we grow older, the mind tends to become caught in repetitive patterns. Then the mind operates imitatively—not creatively—seeing the world the same way day after day after day. In this state of mind, you are not creating anything new because your mind is not exploring new ways of looking at things.

So the problem seems to be how to remove the barriers to creativity that we build as we grow older. We don't need to add something new to ourselves. We just need to find ways to free the creative ability that is already inside us. To give a practical illustration of what I mean, I'd like to talk about something that I think often inhibits the creative process: our tendency to put too many limits on solutions to a problem. What do I mean by too many limits? Look at your handout. There you see nine dots in three rows. Try to draw no more than four straight lines that will touch all nine dots.

Did you solve the problem? You probably had trouble if you were not willing to go outside the limits enclosing the nine dots. Those boundaries are imaginary. Look at this solution.

Students: Wow! I'd never think of that! You've gotta be kidding! It seems so easy now! I got it! Yeah! I got it!

Professor: Great! I'm glad some of you solved the puzzle this way, but there are other solutions, too. Did any of you solve the puzzle in another way? Come on! Don't be shy! No idea is silly as long as it solves the problem. Yes, do you have a solution?

Student 1: Well, you didn't say we had to use only a pen or pencil. So, I cut the dots apart and arranged them in a straight line and then connected them.

Professor: Very original! Anyone else? Any other solutions? Yes, go ahead.

Student 2: How about this: You can tape the handout of the puzzle to a globe and then keep circumnavigating the globe with your pen until you pass through all the dots.

Professor: Wonderful! Very imaginative! Now I have to tell you the solution that my ten-year-old daughter came up with. She solved the problem by using a veeeeery faaaat line! Okay. So now you see how your own mind may put limits on the possible solutions to a problem because you're just seeing things in standard, ordinary ways. The fact of the matter is that to be creative, we have to be able to look at things in extraordinary, new ways.

Obviously, when you try to solve a problem creatively, you first have to figure out what the problem is. Don't state the problem too narrowly, too specifically, or you might limit the number of solutions that you will come up with. Let me give you another practical example of solving a problem creatively. Let's say that your problem is to design a playground. If you think the problem is where to put the playground equipment, you are looking at the problem too narrowly. If you think the problem is both designing the playground equipment and then deciding where to place the equipment, you give yourself a much more creative problem with the possibility for a greater variety of solutions. So I can't emphasize this enough: When you state a problem, don't state it too narrowly or you will see it too narrowly and you will limit the possible solutions.

So, you can see now how our creative abilities can be blocked in a variety of ways. But the real deal is that our culture plays a big part in blocking creative potential. Psychologists say that people here in the United States and Canada seem to have four main cultural blocks to creativity. Let me list them for you. First, we tend to believe that playfulness and humor in problem solving are for children not adults. Second, we tend to think that feelings, intuitions, and pleasure are bad, whereas logic, reason, and numbers are good. Third, most of us think that tradition is better than change. And finally, we believe that scientific thinking and great quantities of money can solve any problem.

Let's go over each of these ideas one at a time. First, despite what you may have heard, humor and creativity are definitely connected. They both open up areas of thought and feeling and connect things or ideas that were never put together before. For example, with a joke—well, wait—let me illustrate. A psychiatrist and a patient are talking and the patient says, "I'm getting really worried about my brother, Doc. He thinks he's a chicken." And the doctor says, "Well, why don't you bring him to me for help?" And the patient answers, "Oh, no. We can't do that." "Why not?" asks the doctor. And the patient answers, "Because we need the eggs."

OK, OK. It's not a great joke, but think about it. You did laugh, so what happened here? You expect that there will be logic to the story and the logic is broken by the surprise punch line "Because we need the eggs" is exactly what makes it funny. The punch line about the eggs was not expected. Creativity is also the appearance of the unexpected. And by the way, there's another connection between humor and creativity. To be creative, you must be willing to be laughed at because we often laugh at the unusual. In fact, many of the important ideas in science were laughed at when they were first presented to the public.

OK, so the next item on our list of cultural blocks to creativity is that reason and logic are better than feelings and intuition. Now, although reason and logic are useful, many great ideas come to people while they are dreaming. In fact, one of the most famous works of the composer Richard Wagner came to him in a dream. So be open to your dreams, imagination, and feelings.

The third thing to consider is tradition versus change. Tradition is valued and worthwhile, but it is often a block to creativity because it represents the ordinary and familiar. The creative process involves things that are new and different. But change is not easy. It takes hard work and great courage. Working for change demands creativity.

And what do you think about the final point—that scientific thinking and lots of money can solve any problem? Yes, in the back, what do you think?

Student 3: Well, I believe that this is true only when scientific thinking is also creative thinking. You know—in the ways you've been telling us about. I also think that the money itself has to be used creatively.

Professor: Yes, very interesting. Let's discuss that further when we have more time.

So, in conclusion, I will summarize what I've said today. Even though the creative process is carried out unconsciously, the reality is that we can still train ourselves to be more creative people. We can do this by removing the limitations we place on ourselves and by becoming aware of any cultural blocks that may inhibit the creative process.

Well, that's all for today. Thank you, and see you next week.

Divulging Information

1 **Listening for Ways of Divulging Information.**   **Page 94.**

Conversation 1
Albert and Bonnie are discussing the real reason that Professor Stone was fired.

Albert:	Did you hear that Professor Stone resigned from his post as president of the Institute of Behavorial Psychology?
Bonnie:	Yeah. I heard that story too.
Albert:	Why do you say it's a story?
Bonnie:	Because I've heard what's really going on. The fact of the matter is that he was forced to quit- fired, in fact.
Albert:	No kidding- why?
Bonnie:	Despite what you believe about him, he doesn't do very careful research and publishes inaccurate data.

Question 1: Is this conversation formal or informal?
Question 2: What phrase helped you decide this?

Conversation 2
Kate and Doug are discussing where Jules got the money for his new motorcycle.

Kate:	Hey, what gives? That's a really fine motorcycle Jules is riding. Where'd he get the cash?
Doug:	I don't know.
Kate:	Oh, come on- what's the scoop?
Doug:	Well, he says he saved up for it, but the real story is: He won the money gambling in Las Vegas and he doesn't want his folks to find out.
Kate:	I thought he told Susie that he couldn't stand Las Vegas.
Doug:	Well, despite what you may have heard, the real story is that he's been sneaking off to Las Vegas just about every other weekend.

Question 1: Is this conversation formal or informal?
Question 2: What phrase helped you decide this?

Focus on Testing. Page 97.

Listen to the two speakers. After each speaker finishes talking, you will hear a question. Circle the letter of the best answer to each question.

Speaker 1

Woman: Let me illustrate my point about creativity. Grandma Moses never had an art lesson in her life and yet her paintings are displayed in art galleries.

Question: What is the speaker implying?

Speaker 2

Man: I really can't emphasize this enough. Creativity is not sex or age linked.

Question: What is the speaker saying?

Chapter 9   Human Behavior

PART 2   **Recognizing Digressions**

Lecture: Group Dynamics

Professor: This afternoon I'm going to talk about a topic that affects every person in this room—group dynamics. Every person in this room is part of some group, right? For example, you belong to this class. And I'm sure that you belong to other groups too, don't you? Your family, right? A social club perhaps? A soccer, golf, or tennis team? The international student association? What else? Help me out.

Student A: Pi Phi sorority.

Student B: Exam study groups.

Student C: Business Students' Discussion Group.

Student D: Volunteers for a Clean Environment.

Student E: Film Club.

Professor: Good. Thanks. At any one time the average person belongs to five or six different groups. A large part of our sense of identity comes from belonging to these groups. In fact, if I asked you to describe yourself, you would probably say, for example, "I'm a student, a basketball player, and a member of the film club," wouldn't you? Well, today we're going to look at two interesting aspects of group dynamics—that is, how groups function. First, we'll look at patterns of communication in groups and then we'll look at how groups affect individual performance.

In groups, communication seems unsystematic, random, and unplanned, doesn't it? Generally, we don't see any pattern of com-

	munication at all. By the way, you all went to the discussion section yesterday, didn't you? Well, what did you notice about the conversations?
Student B:	Everyone kept interrupting me.
Professor:	Yes! And if you were having a good discussion, people kept interrupting each other and talking at the same time, didn't they? I'll bet students talked pretty much whenever they wanted. Well, let's see what researchers have found concerning communication patterns and group dynamics.
	The first pattern they have found occurs in groups where there is a lively discussion. It seems like everyone is talking at once, but actually, only a few people are talking. And it doesn't seem to matter how large the group is—only a few people talk at once. Do you know how many? What do you think?
Student C:	Three? A few is three, right?
Students:	Three? Four? Two?
Professor:	Yes, well, the answer is two. Two people do over 50% of the talking in any group.
	Now let's look at the second pattern researchers found in group dynamics. When we're in a group, sitting around a table perhaps, who do we talk to? As an aside, I must tell you that all the research I know about has been done in the United States and Canada, so the results I have to share with you may only be valid for these countries. Well, as I started to say, who do people talk to when they're sitting together at a table—people across the table, or people sitting next to them?
Students:	Across the table. Next to them.
Professor:	Well, the research shows that in groups of eight or more, people talk to the people sitting across the table from them, not to the people next to them. Why do we talk more to the people sitting opposite us? Probably because in our culture we usually make eye contact with the person we're talking to, and it's not as easy to have eye contact with someone who is sitting next to us. It's much easier to maintain eye contact with someone across the table.
	To go somewhat off the topic for a moment, if you're planning to be a matchmaker and start a romance between two of your friends, don't seat them next to each other at your next dinner party. On second thought, maybe seating them at a corner of the table would be best, wouldn't it? Then they would be very near each other and would only have to turn slightly in order to look into each other's eyes.
	Well, back to business. Now there's one more point that I'd like to mention regarding conversation in groups, and this might be important to the new romance at your dinner party. Who knows? The research also shows that, in general, the person in the group who talks the most is regarded as the leader of the group. However, this person is not usually the most liked in the group, is he? D. J. Stang did some research that showed that the person in the group who talked a moderate amount was liked the most. What use can we make

of this information? A new romance would be affected by this aspect of group dynamics, wouldn't it?

But enough of romance and dinner parties. I now want to discuss another important aspect of group dynamics—the effect a group has on an individual's performance. The research tells us that sometimes the effect of the group on someone's performance is positive, and sometimes it is negative. It took quite a while for social psychologists to figure out why this is true.

Some research showed that people did better on a task when they were doing it in a group. It didn't matter what the task was, whether it was slicing tomatoes or racing bicycles; people just performed better when other people were there. It also didn't matter whether the other people in the group were doing the same task or just watching, so competition was not a factor. The first person to notice this phenomenon was Triplett.

Student A: Excuse me, but what was his first name? It wasn't Tom, was it?

Professor: I'm sorry, I don't remember. Please come by my office if you want the complete reference. Anyway, as I was saying, Triplett's research was done quite a long time ago. In 1898, in fact. He watched bicycle racers and noticed that they did much better when they raced against each other than when they raced only against the clock.

This behavior surprised him, so he conducted a simple experiment. He gave a group of children some fishing poles and string. The children were told to wind the string around the fishing poles as fast as possible. Half of the children worked alone. The others worked in pairs. Interestingly, the children who worked in pairs worked faster than those who worked alone.

Well, you're probably not interested in winding string around fishing poles faster, but you are interested in doing math problems better, aren't you? F. H. Allport had people work on math problems alone and also in groups of five to six. He found that people did better in the group situation than when they worked alone. The theory behind this type of research- research which demonstrates that people do better work in groups—is called social facilitation theory.

Let me digress a bit on this matter of having an audience. In this way, we're like a number of other creatures- ants, for example. Chen did a laboratory experiment with some ants as they were building nests. Chen had some of the ants work alone and some of the ants work with one or two other ants. Guess what! Ants worked harder when they worked with other ants than when they worked alone.

Another famous study was done with cockroaches. Zajonc, Heingartner, and Herman watched cockroaches find their way through a maze while trying to get away from a light. As you may know, cockroaches hate light. They are photophobic, right? The researchers had the cockroaches go through the maze alone and then had them go through the maze with an audience of four other cockroaches. The cockroaches reached the end of the maze faster when they had an audience.

Students:	No way! Really? You're kidding, right?
Professor:	No, No! Really! This is true.

Well, to continue, as I mentioned earlier, there is also research that demonstrates the opposite—that individuals perform worse, not better, on tasks when other people are there! The theory behind this research, which shows that people do poorly in groups, is called social inhibition theory. R. W. Hubbard did an interesting experiment on this. He had people learn a finger maze. This is a maze that you trace with your finger. The people who had an audience did worse than the people who did the maze alone.

So how can we explain these contradictory results? Zajonc finally came up with a possible reason why people sometimes perform better and sometimes worse in front of an audience. He found that the presence of an audience facilitates what you already know how to do. That is, if you *know* what you are doing, having an audience helps you do it better. But if you *don't* already know how to do something, you will probably make some mistakes. And if you have an audience, you will continue to make mistakes. He pointed out that when you are first learning something, you are better off working alone than practicing with other people.

So to recap, the research shows that people generally perform better in groups, except if they are performing a new task. In that case they work better alone. And just let me mention in passing that if you can manage it, you should take tests on a stage in front of a large audience with a group of people who are also taking the test. Not very practical though, is it? And I wonder if it's really true for every task we learn. What do you think? Well let's start with that question next time. See you then.

PART 3 **Using Tag Questions to Ask for Information, Confirm, or Challenge**

---

1 **Listening for Intonation Patterns.**   **Page 108.**

Conversation 1
Steven is telling Tom about the first soccer practice of the season, which is only two days away.

Steven:	Our team is having the first practice of the season this Saturday morning at 8:00. You'll be there, Tom, won't you?
Tom:	Oh sure! I'll be there early.

Question: What intonation pattern does Steven use—genuine question, rhetorical question, or challenging question?

Conversation 2
All week, Steven and Tom have been looking forward to playing soccer on Saturday. Steven is telling a third friend, George, about the practice.

Steven: Our team is having the first practice of the season this Saturday morning at 8:00, George. You'll be there, Tom, won't you?

Tom: Sure will.

Question: What intonation pattern does Steven use this time—genuine question, rhetorical question, or challenging question?

Conversation 3
Soccer practice has been arranged for 6:30 A.M. because another team has reserved the field for 8:30. Tom and Steven are talking about Karl, who told Tom that he wouldn't be coming until 8:00.

Steven: Soccer practice is at 6:30 this Saturday morning because another team has the field at 8:30.

Tom: Steve, Karl told me he couldn't come to soccer practice until eight.

Steven: What a drag. He's always late. He thinks he's coming at eight, does he? Well, I think he's off the team then. He can't come and go as he pleases and still be on the team.

Question: What intonation pattern does Steven use here—genuine question, rhetorical question, or challenging question?

Conversation 4
Charlie's boss expects a report on Friday but realizes that it would be useful at a meeting on Wednesday.

Boss: Charlie, I've got an unexpected merchandising meeting this week. The report won't be done by Wednesday, will it?

Charlie: Well, I don't think so, but we'll work on it.

Question: What intonation pattern does the boss use—genuine question, rhetorical question, or challenging question?

Conversation 5
Josie comes home and sees Peter, one of her housemates, sitting in the living room with his feet up. Since it's already 6:00, she concludes that it's not his turn to cook.

Josie: Hi, Pete. How are you?

Pete: Fine, how 'bout you?

Josie: Good. You're not cooking tonight, huh?

Pete: You got it. It's Bill's turn, right?

Josie: I think so, but he's going to be late again. I know it.

Pete: I think so too. Let's start the soup, OK? Otherwise, it'll be nine o'clock before we ever get anything to eat.

> *Josie:* OK, you're right. I'm starving. You cut the carrots and I'll do the potatoes.

Question : What single-word tag questions are used in this conversation?

Focus on Testing. Page 111.

Listen to the two conversations. After each conversation, you will hear a question. Circle the letter of the best answer to each question.

Conversation 1

> *Billy:* This looks like the right size tennis racket, doesn't it? Try a few out. I'm going to look at the golf clubs.
>
> *Alex:* You'll come back and help me with this in a few minutes, won't you?
>
> *Billy:* Sure. Just as soon as I pick out a new driver.

Question: Where does this conversation take place?

Conversation 2

> *Man:* Tom can get enough votes to win the election, can't he?
>
> *Woman:* Well, if he gets the Asian, the African American, and the Native American special-interest groups on his side, he can't lose, can he?

Question: What is the woman saying?

Chapter 10 Crime and Punishment

PART 2 **Paraphrasing**

Lecture: Human Choice: Predetermination or Free Will?

> *Professor:* OK, let's get started. Today's lecture about choice is in two parts. The first part of the lecture is about the difference between predetermination and free will. I hope that by the end of class that difference will be clear to you all, because I want to hear your ideas on these two very different views of the world.
>
> The second part of the lecture is about choice in the real world—when life-or-death decisions have to be made.
>
> So, do you believe that our lives are predetermined or do you believe that we make choices that direct our lives? Basically, if you believe that our lives are predetermined, then you believe that everything we do is decided before we are born. Maybe you think we are

programmed to do the things we do. Or perhaps you think a spiritual force makes all our decisions for us. But even if we believe our lives are somehow predetermined, we still appear to be making choices every day. We choose what to have for dinner or what movie to go to. We choose our friends from among the hundreds of people we meet. So the question is: are these really choices, or is the concept of free choice only an illusion?

On the other hand, if you believe that we have free will, then you believe that we do really make all our own decisions. For example, the Hindus and Buddhists believe that our choices are made freely and that these choices add up to either a good life or a bad life. This is called karma. They also believe in reincarnation. According to this belief, if we don't make enough good decisions during one lifetime, we are reborn to try to do better in the next life.

These two opposing views, predetermination and free will, can have important effects on our lives. How do you think they can affect us? Yes, Craig?

Student 1: Well, if you believe that everything is predetermined . . . then that might make you feel as if you have no control over what happens to you . . . you know . . . no control over your life.

Student 2: And that feeling would certainly affect your behavior. For example, maybe you would feel that if you are not in control, then you don't have to take responsibility for your choices.

Professor: Yes, that's quite possible. Therefore, we should examine these opposing views about choice as a starting point in determining our own attitude toward life. You may recall that Socrates suggested this when he said that the "unexamined life is not worth living."

How many of you have looked at your past actions and said, "I wish I had done that differently" or "If only I had decided to do this instead of what I did"? And certainly we all have worried about the future and thought, "I hope I can do the right thing." Our relationship to the past and to the future seems to be connected with our present choices. That is, all our wishes and hopes for the future are very connected to what we choose now, in the present.

Stop 1

Professor: Now let's talk about choice in the real world. The practical implications of choice increase and intensify when life-or-death decisions have to be made. For example, if you were a judge and your job was to sentence a person to prison or even death for violation of rules or beliefs in your community, you might question the nature of right and wrong before finally reaching a decision. Do any of you recall the character Jean Valjean from *Les Miserables*, who was sentenced to seven years of slavery for stealing a loaf of bread for his starving family? What choice would you have made if you were the judge? I hope you would consider all the possible choices.

Students: Wow. That's a tough one. I don't know. I'm really not sure. I need to think about it.

Professor:	And what if you were Jean Valjean? Would you have chosen to break the law to feed your family?
Students:	Absolutely! Of course! I'd have to! You bet your life I would!

Stop 2

Professor:	OK. All right then. But now I want you to think about this. Would you then say that you were not really responsible for the crime? Would you try to get off by saying you did it because the society did not provide a job for you and that's why you and your family were so hungry? This is not an easy question, is it?
	Now, what about this case? On March 30, 1981, the president of the United States, Ronald Reagan, and three other men were shot on a street in Washington, D. C. John Hinckley Jr., the young man who shot these men, admitted that he felt no remorse about his crime. Three of his four victims recovered; the fourth suffered permanent brain damage.
	Fifteen months later, after an eight-week trial that cost $3 million, Hinckley was found "not guilty by reason of insanity." Think about that. Hinckley shot the president of the United States and three other people and was only sent to a mental hospital for counseling and treatment. When the psychiatrists decide that he is well enough, he will be released and sent home. He will not go to prison.
Student 1:	Wow! That's incredible!
Student 2:	That's terrible!
Student 3:	No kidding! I didn't know that!
Professor:	Well, it's true. Naturally, many people were very angry that Hinkley received such a small punishment. However, Hinckley's punishment is not my focus here. I want to focus instead on the choice Hinckley made. His actions came from his choice, and his actions injured four people.
	Did you know that in the United States, only those criminals who made their choices consciously, willfully, and freely are punished? Yup, that's the law. If it is proven in court that an act, no matter how evil, was caused by influences beyond the control of the person who did it, then that person is not punished for the act.
	In other words, in our society, the law says that you are not responsible for choices you make if you are not aware or in control of your actions. This is called legal insanity. How about that!

Stop 3

Professor:	We are faced with other questions—perhaps not as serious—every moment of our lives. Who will I go out with on Saturday night? Shall I go on a diet? Should I go to the movies tonight or should I study for that biology test? Should I make long-range plans for my career? And more important, how should I treat other people?
	The poetry, fiction, and theater of every culture reflect the drama involved in making these kinds of choices, but they do not offer simple answers. The only definite rule we are given about making choices is that we have to make them or they will be made for us. Ah, but

if only we could make perfect choices, then there would be no problem, right?

In summary, we have touched lightly on the extremely important matter of the nature of human choice and briefly examined the relationship between human choice, crime, and punishment. I hope this lecture has stimulated you to reflect on your own choices—what they are and why you are making them—and to consider how they shape your worldview and what your responsibility is for their effects. And remember: whether you think your choices are predetermined or made freely, you cannot get away from making choices, for after all, to choose is to be human.

Stop 4

Expressing Wishes, Hopes, and Desires

1 **Listening for Wishes, Hopes, and Desires.   Page 120.**

Laura:	Have you found a house to rent yet?
James:	No, not yet. I hope I find one soon. My family is arriving in a few days, and I want to have a house ready for them when they get here.
Laura:	Sounds like you could use some help.
James:	Well, maybe a little, but probably all I really need is more money. If only I didn't have to find something inexpensive. I wish I were making more money. Then I would have more choices of houses.
Laura:	Well, I may be able to help you out there.
James:	You mean you know of a good house for us?
Laura:	Not exactly. But I might know of a way for you to make some easy money making some quick deliveries.
James:	Uh-oh. This sounds too easy to be legal. But I tell you, I'm getting really desperate at this point. I just might be tempted anyway.
Laura:	Well, I certainly hope you're just kidding. But this time you don't have to worry. It's definitely legal. I heard that Pizza Time wants someone to deliver pizzas from 6:00 to 9:00 every night. And the pay's not bad.
James:	Oh, is that all? Well, that sounds great! Who do I talk to?

Focus on Testing. Page 123.

Listen to the two conversations. After each conversation, you will hear a question. Circle the letter of the best answer to each question.

Conversation 1

Allan:	My brother almost stole a car once.
Emily:	Allan, you're kidding! How did you stop him?

| Allan: | I asked him, "Do you want to go to jail?" And he said, "No." Then I told him, "If you can't do the time, don't do the crime." |
| Emily: | That's great. I bet the thought of time in jail changed his mind. |

Question: What was Allan saying to his brother?

Conversation 2

| Maria: | Oh, Carla. I wish I were rich and famous. |
| Carla: | Are you sure that's what you want, Maria? There's an old saying: be careful what you wish for because you might get it. |

Question: What is Carla trying to tell Maria?

Chapter 11 The Physical World

PART 2   Outlining

Lecture: Penguins at the Pole

Professor Gill:	Good morning.
Class:	Good morning.
Professor Gill:	Well, to continue with our study of polar ecosystems, I've arranged a special treat for you today. I've invited Professor Byrd, who has just returned from a two-year field study in Antarctica, to come and speak with us. He's going to share a few things about a part-time polar resident—the penguin.
Professor Byrd:	Hello. I see that you're all smiling. It never fails! Every time people hear that my lecture will be about penguins, everyone immediately seems more cheerful. This is not surprising, seeing as how no one can resist these awkward little creatures that appear to be dressed in black and white suits.

Well, to begin. Antarctica is like a huge and desolate icy desert and only the strongest forms of life survive there. It seems strange that this harsh land could be the spring and summer home of a migratory bird—the penguin.

Did I say bird? It also seems strange to call something that cannot fly a bird. But that's not all! The penguin is a tireless swimmer and is also affectionate, considerate, and loyal—rare qualities in the bird kingdom. On account of these characteristics, these delightful creatures are thought of as treasures of the Antarctic.

The penguin is an extremely important part of this very limited ecosystem. In the Antarctic, all the activity of the ecosystem takes place on a thin shelf of land next to the great dome of ice that covers most of the region. It is here, to this little bit of beachfront, that the penguin comes to mate and raise babies. It would be a little cold for us at this beach, though.

The Adelie penguin arrives with the relative warmth of spring, when the temperature rises above zero degrees Fahrenheit. That would be at about minus seventeen degrees Celsius. Right away the penguin begins a long fast, a period in which it does not eat. During the previous months, the penguins continuously ate shrimp and small fish in warmer water, and they now have a store of fat to carry them through the months ahead. Owing to these fat reserves, they are able to swim hundreds of miles to the familiar ground of the desolate Antarctic shore.

When the penguins arrive at the nesting ground, their first task is to pair up—to mate—and to begin a kind of "civilized" life. Since as many as 50,000 birds may gather at a time, there is definitely a need for order and neatness. Because of this need, penguins build nests in such perfect rows that the nesting area looks like the streets of a city.

However, this order is often interrupted by battles between birds. For example, two male birds may fight a small war over a particularly adorable female. Or a male and female may battle as they settle the marriage contract. These little battles go on constantly for several weeks, until the pairs, or mates, are settled. The penguins never actually kill one another, but it is not unusual to see bloodstains and broken wings. The winners of these love battles have won a relationship with a female that is the most extraordinary in the animal world. There seems to be a blissful understanding between the mates. I've observed the delicate and kind way they treat each other, at times standing very close and swaying back and forth as if dancing to celebrate their marriage. The losers, the males that fail to find a suitable mate, move to the edge of the nesting ground. These birds become the "hooligans," or delinquents, of the group. They steal unguarded eggs, disturb nests, and play jokes on the happy couples.

Student 1: I think we have a few of those hooligan types in this class.

All Students: (laughter)

Professor Byrd: Yes, I've seen that behavior myself. So . . . After nearly a month of fasting, the eggs are laid in little nests made of stones by the males. Then family life begins. Although the brooding instinct is very strong and parental care is truly dedicated, as many as 75% of the eggs are lost due to catastrophic floods, death of the parents, destruction of the nests by landslides or heavy snows, bad behavior of the "hooligan" males I mentioned before, or of course, the eggs being eaten by other birds.

Class: That's awful! That's so sad! Oh, no!

Professor Byrd: Yes, it's sad, but some eggs do survive, of course, and once the chicks begin to hatch out of the eggs, the penguin colony teems with life. The long fast is over, and the parents take turns feeding and bringing back food for the new penguin chick.

It is during this period that the comical character of the penguin is revealed. They often feed in large groups, walking or sliding for miles in single file lines to the ocean. There they dare one another to jump into the water. They often approach the edge of a cliff and then retreat several times.

Once one brave penguin dives in, however, the others follow almost at once, leaping from exactly the same spot. In the water, they play various water sports that they've invented while they stuff themselves with shrimp and other small sea creatures.

It's not all fun and games, however. Even though their black and white color helps hide them, there is not very much the penguins can do to protect themselves from the jaws of the sea leopard. This scary creature looks like a cross between a seal and a great white shark. Some of you might remember the movie *Jaws*?

Class: Yeah! Sure! Right!

Student 1: Sure we do! Dah-dum, dah-dum, dah-dum.

Professor Byrd: Well, the sea leopard jaw is just as tough! The sea leopard is a very big seal with many large, sharp teeth, an aggressive disposition, and a taste for penguin meat. Even though penguins are excellent swimmers, it is difficult for them to escape these ferocious attackers.

For this reason, the group of penguins is smaller when it returns to the nesting ground the next spring. But penguins are generous creatures and food is shared with the orphaned chicks—those whose parents have not returned. Adult penguins also share babysitting duties. One bird will watch over several chicks while the others play.

Student 2: Even the males?

Professor Byrd: Especially the males!

Student 2: Hear that, Frank?

Professor Byrd: Oh, yes. Penguins share everything. And they love to visit with neighbors, explore nearby ice floes, and even climb mountains, following the leader in long lines up the mountainside.

When the mating season finally comes to an end, the penguins line up in rows like little black and white soldiers and prepare to march to the sea. At a signal that humans cannot perceive, the penguins suddenly begin their orderly walk. At the edge of the sea, they stand as if at attention again, waiting for another signal. When it is given, they begin their swim to their winter home on another part of the continent.

Well, I think I'm keeping you a bit late. If Professor Gill will invite me back maybe we can continue talking about penguins another time.

Class: Yes! That's would be great! Please come back!

Professor Gill: Definitely. I think that can be arranged. Thank you so much, Professor Byrd. We've all enjoyed your talk tremendously.

PART 3   Stating Reasons

1   Listening for Ways to State Reasons.   Page 131.

Sarah: Hello?

John: Hello. Sarah? This is John.

Sarah: John! Hello! How nice to hear from you. I thought you'd left to do your field study already.

John: No, not yet. We ran into a few problems. Some of our specialized equipment hasn't arrived yet. On account of this we may have to put off the field study until next year.

Sarah: I'm sorry to hear that, but couldn't you leave as soon as the equipment arrives?

John: Well, ordinarily we might, but in view of the fact that the field study was to be in Antarctica, there's yet another problem.

Sarah: Really? What's that?

John: Well, it's almost winter there now, and since our study will take several months, we'll have to wait at least until next spring. It's just too cold to do much outdoor study there in the winter.

Sarah: Well, it's too bad about having to cancel your trip, but since you're still in town, why don't you come over for a visit tonight?

John: I was hoping you'd say that! I'd love to.

PART 4   Focus on Testing. Page 133.

Listen to the two conversations. After each conversation, you will hear a question. Circle the letter of the best answer to each question.

Conversation 1

College dean: Since you won't be joining the Antarctica expedition this year, would you reconsider our offer to join the staff here at Elmhurst?

Explorer: Thank you again for the offer, Dean Hemmings, but the reason I refused still holds. I just don't think I'm cut out for teaching.

Question: What is the man refusing?

Conversation 2

Man: In view of the fact that people are ignoring the importance of the ecology of the polar regions, I think we're headed for catastrophe.

Woman: Oh, you mean like a worldwide drought caused by global warming or severe flooding in coastal cities?

Question: What is the man implying?

Chapter 12 Together on a Small Planet

PART 2   Summarizing

Lecture: Folk Wisdom

Professor: Let's see. Today we're going to be talking about folk wisdom.

Every culture has many sayings that give advice about life. These sayings are part of what is commonly called folk wisdom. Of course, folk wisdom is also expressed in other ways, such as myths, fairy tales, legends, and songs. Often, however, folk wisdom is shared in the form of short sayings about the best ways to approach life's joys and sorrows.

Today, we'll look at some of the humorous sayings of three famous Americans: Benjamin Franklin, Abraham Lincoln, and Mark Twain. Then I'll ask you to share some examples of folk wisdom from your own communities.

One characteristic of American folk wisdom is its humor. Humor makes the bitter medicine of life easier to swallow. It sometimes makes the harsh realities of life more attractive. For example, Ben Franklin's clever saying, "A full belly makes a dull brain" means "People who are well-fed or self-satisfied can become lazy and stupid." But this paraphrasing loses the elegance and humor of Franklin's original saying. Some moralists in the United States are successful because they are able to say wise things humorously.

And Ben Franklin was the first of many Americans to be admired for his humorous folk wisdom. Franklin himself loved to have fun. He liked to eat a lot, drink a lot, and be merry, but he always told others to practice moderation. For example, he said, "Early to bed and early to rise makes a man healthy, wealthy, and wise."

Franklin wrote a book called *Poor Richard's Almanac* that is filled with good ideas on how to live a happy but moderate life. For example, he advised, "Keep your eyes wide open before marriage and half-shut afterwards" and "Three may keep a secret if two of them are dead." He also wrote, "Nothing is more fatal to health than overcare of it." Franklin's style was sensible, easy, simple, and colloquial.

Abraham Lincoln expressed similar opinions about life but in a different way. Lincoln continued the tradition of "horse sense" humor that was begun by Davy Crockett, who was called the "coonskin philosopher" because of the raccoon-skin cap he always wore. Horse sense is truth expressed in simple terms. "Make sure you're right, then go ahead" is a quote from Crockett. This type of humor appeals to people who are hungry for practical common sense.

Lincoln understood the need for horse sense. He was both a politician and an idealist, and he knew how to use common sense to influence people's opinions. He could take the highest moral principles or the most critical observations and use them in folksy—or simple commonsense—humor to make them better understood and more easily accepted. Take, for example, this quote, which is one of best known in the United States: "You can fool all of the people some of the time, and some of the people all of the time, but you can't fool all of the people all of the time." Another of Lincoln's wise, folksy statements is: "The Lord prefers common-looking people. That is why he makes so many of them."

There is no doubt that people need a little push sometimes to help them see the folly of their ways. Mark Twain used humor to reveal that many popular ideas were false, foolish, or even harmful. Twain thought that most human beings didn't examine why they believed certain things, and that they were too easily influenced by the opinions of people in power. He felt that it was easier for people to be "misled" than to be led correctly, so he tried to show the foolishness of those in power. For example, he said, "Hain't we got all the fools in town on our side and ain't that a big enough majority in any town?"

People in power often use statistics to try to prove their points, and Twain had a comment to make about this too. He said, "There are three kinds of lies—lies, damned lies, and statistics." Like Franklin and Lincoln, Twain also gave good advice. He said, for example, "It is by the goodness of God that we have in our country three precious things: freedom of speech, freedom of conscience, and the prudence never to practice either." This is quite a strong statement on how to get along with other people.

After reading a small sample of Twain, you might get the impression that he was a misanthrope, a person who saw everyone's mistakes and never noticed their good qualities. It's true that his humor was sometimes harsh, but it was used to reveal truths about human relationships. Twain thought the result would be a better, more just society. However, he also realized that he irritated a lot of people. He was aware that when newspapers reported his death, many people might be happy to hear the news. The telegram he sent from Europe to the Associated Press is typical of his humor. It read, "The reports of my death are greatly exaggerated."

Well, now. The students in this class come from a lot of different backgrounds. How about sharing with the group some of the sayings, some of the folk wisdom, from your culture? Dimitri, what about starting with you? Can you give us a saying from Greece?

Dimitri: Well . . . Here's one: "The beginning is half of every action."

Professor: That's certainly true. Just getting started is often the hardest part. Nandini, do you know any Hindu sayings?

Nandini: Oh, yes: "It's no sin to kill the killer." But, actually, I don't agree with this saying.

Professor: That's definitely a good discussion topic. Brigitta, what about the Dutch?

Brigitta: I really like this one: we say, "Nobody's sweetheart is ugly." In English you say, "Love is blind," right?

Professor:	That's right. Dan, can you tell us a Native American saying that you really like?
Dan:	You probably know this one: "Don't judge a man until you have walked two moons in his moccasins."
Brigitta:	What are moccasins?
Dan:	They're a kind of shoe.
Brigitta:	Oh, now I see.
Professor:	Yes, I have heard that one, Dan. Thank you. Mohammed, what about you?
Mohammed:	If a camel once gets his nose in the tent, his body will follow.
Professor:	That's great! I had never heard that one. Keiko, do you have a favorite folk saying from your country?
Keiko:	Yes, I do. "To kick with a sore toe only hurts the foot."
Professor:	I had never heard that one either. It makes a lot of sense. And who's left? Ahmet. How about a Turkish saying?
Ahmet:	Well, we love coffee, you know. So we say: "Coffee should be as black as hell, as strong as death, and as sweet as love."
Professor:	Oh, yes. Very good. Well, that's all we have time for. Now as you work on your presentations, remember what Mark Twain said, "It takes more than three weeks to prepare a good impromptu speech."

PART 3	**Telling a Joke**

---

1 **Listening for Expressions that Introduce Jokes.** **Page 143.**

Jimmy:	Hi, guys. What's up?
Frank:	Oh, nothing. We're just sitting around having coffee, telling jokes.
Catherine:	Yeah, like the one my teacher told in education class. Once there was a teacher who was telling about how machines help people and she asked a student, "John, can you name a great timesaver?" "Yes," John replied. "Love at first sight."
Jimmy:	Oh, Catherine, that's funny. I've spent a lot of time in New York, and I love to tell the one about the boy who asked for directions to a famous concert hall. "Sir," he asked an old gentleman, "How do you get to Carnegie Hall?" The old man replied, "Practice, practice, practice."
Catherine:	You groaned the loudest, Joanna, so you go next.
Joanna:	Have you heard the one about the man who was dining in an expensive restaurant and the waiter came by and asked, "How did you find your steak, sir?" and the man answered, "Purely by accident. I moved the potatoes and the peas, and there it was."
Frank:	I like the one about the little girl who was asked, "Sally, when you get as big as your mother, what will you do?" and Sally answered quite seriously, "Diet."
Jimmy:	Hey, you guys. Enough of this. I've got to go study.

Catherine: Me too. See you guys later.

     All: Bye. See you later. Have a good one.

Question 1: Catherine tells a joke that she heard her teacher tell. How does Catherine introduce the joke?

Question 2: Jimmy tells a joke about a boy in New York City. How does Jimmy introduce his joke?

Question 3: Joanna tells a joke about a man in a restaurant. How does Joanna introduce her joke?

Question 4: Frank tells a joke about a little girl. How does Frank introduce the joke?

<table>
<tr><td>PART 4</td></tr>
</table>

Focus on Testing. Page 145.

Listen to the two conversations. After each conversation, you will hear a question. Circle the letter of the best answer to each question.

Conversation 1

    Norm: Julie, have you heard the one about the two penguins having a drink at a bar?

    Julie: Oh no, Norm. Not another weird joke.

    Norm: OK, how about the one about the chicken and the duck?

    Julie: No, no. Gimme a break.

Question: Why is Julie refusing to listen to Norman?

Conversation 2

    Harold: I'm not sure whether I should tell that story about Mr. Leonard at the awards dinner. What do you think?

    Susan: Well, you're a good storyteller, but I'm not sure people would find it all that interesting.

    Harold: What are you trying to say, Susan?

    Susan: In sum, when in doubt, leave it out.

Question: What does Susan mean?

Acknowledgments

First we wish to acknowledge the expertise, imagination, and inspiration of our editor, Annie Sullivan, whose incredible humor, dedication, and multiple talents contributed so much to this edition. She rocks! We also wish to express our deepest appreciation to Tina Carver at McGraw-Hill for pursuing this fourth edition and treating us with style. The skills, ideas, and creativity of Marilyn Bernstein, Steven Carlson, Jill Wagner-Schimpff, Steven Hollander, Judy Tanka, and Steven Marx who worked on the first three editions laid the foundation for the fourth. We are indebted to Erik Børve for publishing the ground-breaking first edition and grateful to Mary McVey Gill for her efforts in gathering the original team, her excellent editorial work, and her friendship.

We are also grateful to others who have provided creative suggestions and other support. Steve Aron, Connie Bendal, Mary, Louise, and Elizabeth Dunn; Annie Gardiner, Sue Garfield; Osha Hanfling, Alan Kaiser, Dean Lerner, Eliot Levinson, David Marimont; Manouso Manos, Andreas Paecpke, DeeDee Quinn; John Schumacher, Ann Stromberg; Pat Sutton; Nancy Van Gundy, Patricia Walden and of course the folks down at the Plant: Alice, Joe Bankman, Gray Clossman, Peter Detkin, Barbara Fried, Frank Koenig, Michelle Oastes, Greg and Dorit Scharff, Barr and Susan Taylor, and David Yohai.

We thank the staff at the Palo Alto Public Library and San Francisco State University for their assistance and support.

Photo Credits

Page 1 ©Mark Richards/Photo Edit; *Page 2* ©Christopher Johnson/Stock Boston; *Page 7* ©Frank Pedrick/The Image Works; *Page 9* ©Darlene Gottfried/The Image Works; *Page 12* ©Rudi Von Briel/Photo Edit; *Page 17* ©Joseph Skuyler/Stock Boston; *Page 21* ©Will Hart/Photo Edit; *Page 23* ©Myrleen Cate/Photo Edit; *Page 25* ©K. Preuss/The Image Works; *Page 27* ©Stephen Frisch/Stock boston *Page 29* ©Ellen Senisi/The Image Works; *Page 30* ©Michael Newman/Photo Edit; *Page 34* ©Novastock/Photo Edit; *Page 35* ©Elizabeth Crews/Stock Boston; *Page 41* ©Tom Prettyman/Photo Edit; *Page 42* left ©Nance Trueworthy, right ©Superstock Images; *Page 46* ©Superstock Images; *Page 47* ©Bonnie Kamin/Photo Edit; *Page 48* ©Photo Edit; *Page 51* ©Courtesy of NASA; *Page 52* ©Courtesy of NASA; *Page 57* ©Courtesy of NASA; *Page 60* ©Courtesy of NASA; *Page 63* ©Erik De Castro/Reuters/Archive Photos; *Page 64* ©Superstock Images; *Page 67* ©Sean Prague/Stock Boston; *Page 71* ©Francene Keary/Stock Boston; *Page 75* ©Charles Plattiau/Archive Photos; *Page 76* ©Hulton-Deutsh/Corbis; *Page 79* ©Reuters New Media Inc./Corbis; *Page 80* ©Corbis; *Page 82* ©Michael Newman/Photo Edit; *Page 87* ©Jerry Howard/Stock Boston; *Page 88* ©Brian Haimer/Photo Edit; *Page 91* ©Bettman/Corbis; *Page 93* all four photos ©Photo Edit; *Page 95* Courtesy of Christie's Images; *Page 97* ©Michael Dwyer/Stock Boston; *Page 99* ©David Young Wolf/Photo Edit; *Page 100* left ©Michael Dwyer/Stock Boston, right ©Frederick D. Bodin/Stock Boston; *Page 106* ©Syracuse Newspapers/The Image Works; *Page 108* ©David Young Wolf/Photo Edit; *Page 110* ©Corbis; *Page 113* ©Bob Daemmrich/The